THE BIBLE *and* FLYING SAUCERS

THE BIBLE AND FLYING SAUCERS

by

Barry H. Downing

J. B. LIPPINCOTT COMPANY

PHILADELPHIA and NEW YORK

TO KATHLEEN

With faith, hope, and love

PREFACE

In order to be a scientist, one must be willing to make observations. Scientists make tremendous efforts to build telescopes so that they can see great distances into space, or electron microscopes so that they can observe minute structures. Scientists construct all kinds of instruments such as voltmeters and oscilloscopes so that they can observe the invisible.

Scientists want to look at the evidence. I think that there are probably many reasons why we would rather not look at the evidence which suggests that there may be a relation between the Biblical religion and flying saucers. But I believe that the time has come when it will be worth

our while to begin to make careful observations concerning the Biblical view of the universe and our presently
emerging view of the universe.

Walter Sullivan's book *We Are Not Alone* is not a book
about flying saucers, but rather, an account of how the
history of science has led us up to our present search for
life in space. Even apart from the idea of flying saucers,
modern science now seems quite convinced that man is
not alone in the universe. In all probability there is life on
many planets throughout the universe; civilizations may
have begun space travel long before men began to venture
above the surface of the earth.

What does this have to do with the Biblical religion?
Modern theology, such as the "death of God" theology, is
based on the assumption that many of the Biblical reports
are mythological—make-believe. Included in Biblical
mythology was the belief that the Biblical people were
frequently visited by superior beings from another world.
Theologians who demythologize these beings—often
called angels, or messengers—do so in the name of modern
science. It is not clear to me how we can demythologize
the Biblical material in the name of science when in fact
modern science seems quite convinced that in all probability there are in the universe many advanced civilizations involved in space travel. We cannot begin our Biblical studies with the assumption that the Biblical people
were *not* visited by superior beings from another world;
at least we cannot do so in the name of modern science.

Furthermore, we do have the problem of flying saucers
with us, and if they exist, we cannot be sure how long an
advanced civilization may have been observing our life

on earth. We might have to think in terms of an entirely different time scale for such a civilization: a thousand years might be like a day. Consequently, we really should look at the Biblical material and try to discover what the beings from another world were reported to have done.

The heart of the Old Testament religion is the Exodus, which reported that something resembling a space vehicle —a "pillar of cloud by day, and pillar of fire by night"— led the Hebrew people out of Egypt up to the "Red Sea," hovered over the sea while it parted, and then led them into the wilderness, where an "angel" proceeded to give them religious instructions. The fact that some sort of Unidentified Flying Object—UFO—was reported to have been present at the Red Sea at the time of the parting should cause us to desire a closer look. The parting of the sea was, of course, in itself unique—so much so, in fact, that we should think seriously about the outside force reported to have been present at the time of the parting. I personally find the suggestion that the parting of the Red Sea was deliberately caused by intelligent beings in some sort of space vehicle to be the most persuasive explanation available at the present time.

There are other parts of this book which I believe are less credible, including some of my speculations concerning the relation between Einstein's theory of relativity and the existence of heaven. I am not an authority on Einstein or on heaven, and I hope I can be forgiven where I have misrepresented both. But modern theology has argued that we must take the results of the physical sciences seriously, and with this I agree, provided we remember the basically tentative nature of most scientific statements. Yet while modern theologians have said that we must pay heed to the physical sciences, these same theologians have mainly been absorbed in the psychological and social sciences.

From what I observe concerning the beliefs of modern science about space and about the universe, and the Biblical beliefs about the universe, aside from the fact that the Biblical language is not technically oriented, it appears to me that the relationship between these two world views is still quite open. This book is an attempt to place the world of the Bible and our world of space travel, flying saucers, and relativity theory side by side and observe any relationships between the two worlds. Our conclusions about what we see may be tentative, but it is still scientific to look.

I wish to thank those who have helped, directly or indirectly, with this book. The idea for the manuscript germinated during my last year of study at the University of Edinburgh, New College, in Scotland. During this period I was involved in an examination of Biblical and scientific concepts of space under the supervision of Professor John McIntyre and Professor T. F. Torrance. This manuscript was written after I returned to the United States, so that neither Professor McIntyre nor Professor Torrance has seen it, and yet without the background I received in Edinburgh this book would not have been written. I am very much indebted to both men for their time and advice in the past, although they can in no way be blamed for the ideas or errors in this book.

I am indebted to Dr. James M. Boice for his long friendship and for his willingness to read the manuscript, as well as to the Reverend Charles G. Harris for his evaluation of the manuscript, and to the Reverend George M. Rynick not only for his discussion of the manuscript, but also for his encouragement in seeking publication.

I have sought advice concerning modern concepts of relativity from Dr. William Rodgers, have discussed the mathematical problems of space topology with Mr. David Andersen, and have received assistance from Mr. David Schrader in the collection of material concerning flying saucers. I am also indebted to my in-laws, the Reverend and Mrs. T. A. Schrader, for their support while I was writing the manuscript, and to my parents, Mr. and Mrs. Franklin Downing, who have long encouraged my studies, and who listened patiently while I read the manuscript to them. Finally, of course, I am indebted most to the person to whom this book is dedicated—my wife, who supported me during three years of seminary study at Princeton, encouraged me to take on further study in Edinburgh which often did not appear to be bearing fruit, and aside from all this has been a good wife and mother.

B. H. D.

CONTENTS

THE BIBLE *and* FLYING SAUCERS

CHAPTER I

SPACE AND THE BIBLE

WHAT?—THE BIBLE AND FLYING SAUCERS?

Before you become either extremely angry or even more extremely amused because someone is attempting to link together the Bible and flying saucers, consider the following:[1] *

(1) We live in an age in which theologians (men who are supposed to be on God's side) are writing about the "death of God."[2] This makes some people angry and others laugh, and I can sympathize with both emotions. I think, however, that it is no more ridiculous to talk about the relation between the Bible and flying saucers than it is to describe God's funeral.

* Superior numerals refer to the Notes at the end of the text.

(2) To those who have read their Bibles I now raise the following question: Why do angels make so many appearances in the Bible? The "death of God" theologians say that angels are, so to speak, "make believe"; they are "mythological"—angels do not really exist. But the Bible argues—in effect—that the angels *caused* the religion of the Bible, under God's direction. Consider the following. Suppose that in five hundred years humans on earth should advance technologically in the space age to the point where we were to travel to another world in a space ship and discover intelligent beings who were scientifically primitive. Suppose that Christian missionaries were to travel in space to this planet to try to convert these primitive people to Christianity. How would these people talk about our missionaries? The Bible seems to suggest that angels are very much like missionaries from another world.

(3) It is true that I do not have absolute proof that flying saucers exist, but so many people have seen—or claim to have seen—flying saucers that the term is commonplace. I do not even need to define what flying saucers are. Even if they do not exist, everyone knows what they are! But I believe there is a good possibility that flying saucers do exist, and that they carry intelligent beings from another world. Could these be the same "missionaries" who started the Biblical religion? You certainly have the right at this point to answer, "Of course not; it is impossible." I can understand how impossible it must seem, but I have found the evidence extremely interesting.

The central event in the Old Testament is the Exodus; the Hebrew people were slaves in Egypt, so the Bible reports, and God sent an "angel" to Moses and called him to lead the Israelites out of Egypt. After various plagues came upon the Egyptians, the Israelites escaped, and for the next forty years "the Lord went before them by day in a pillar of cloud to lead them along the way, and by night in a pillar of fire to give them light, that they might travel by day and by night" (Exodus 13:21). This strange aerial object looked cloudlike during the day and glowed in the dark, a description often associated with modern flying saucers. Eventually this strange "cloud" seemed to defeat the Egyptians in battle; it gave guidance and instructions to Moses, and this "angel" from God even provided Moses with the Ten Commandments. However unlikely it may seem, the Bible reports that during the central event of the Old Testament—the Exodus—some kind of space object was always present, and the Biblical people believed that this object was sent from another world. We will investigate the activity of this "pillar of cloud" in greater detail in Chapter III.

The New Testament focuses on the person of a man named Jesus, who is recorded to have said, "You are from below, I am from above; you are of this world, I am not of this world" (John 8:23). Jesus often claimed to have come from another world; he is reported to have had contact with beings from another world, such as during his Resurrection from the dead. He accepted the teaching of Moses, and claimed to be part of a whole plan which included the Old Testament religion. After Jesus had finished his ministry on earth, the Bible reports that he was taken off into space in something which might be a space vehicle. The disciples were gathered with Jesus on the Mount of Olives just outside Jerusalem, and when he finished speaking "as they [the disciples] were looking on, he was lifted up, and a cloud took him out of their sight" (Acts 1:9).

But how could Jesus have been taken off into space in a cloud? The way the Bible speaks about the life of Jesus certainly makes one suspect that his whole life is a highly improbable story. How gullible can a scientifically minded twentieth-century person be? We would not expect an ordinary human being to do the things Jesus did. But the Bible maintains that Jesus was not an ordinary human being. He did not come from our world; he came from another world, and eventually he returned to that world in a "cloud." Once Jesus asked, "Then what if you were to see the Son of man ascending where he was before?" (John 6:62) Ordinary white, fluffy cumulus clouds do not carry people off into space. In the space age I believe that we are compelled to ask: Was this an ordinary cloud, or was this the way the Bible described some sort of space vehicle? This ascension "cloud" is one example of many "Unidentified Flying Objects" (UFOs) which are described in the Bible. There is no reason to expect Biblical people to call a flying saucer a flying saucer even if they saw one. But if they should have contact with a flying saucer, what would they call it? A "cloud"? We do not really believe that flying saucers get up from our dinner tables and carry people about; I do not think that the Biblical people believed that ordinary clouds carry people about in space. What we have to do is to study the Biblical UFOs; we shall discover that just as UFO is a "short" form for Unidentified Flying Object, so a "cloud" is the Bible's "short" form for some sort of space vehicle which seems to look and operate very much like modern flying saucers.

But one has the right to ask, "If there is such an obvious relation between the Bible and flying saucers, why has not this possibility received serious theological attention long before now?" Flying saucers have been reported for several years. Why has no careful theological study been made?

One obvious reason is that the existence of flying saucers is highly suspect. If they do not exist, then they cannot have much of a relation to the Bible. Furthermore, it is often falsely assumed that flying saucers are a post-World War II phenomenon, so that one would suppose that this "new" phenomenon could not have anything to do with an ancient religion. Another reason is that even if the existence of flying saucers were proved beyond reasonable doubt, the present state of theology presents a serious barrier to an immediate study of a possible relation between the Bible and flying saucers. Modern theology assumes that the various beings from another world discussed in the Bible are "mythological," make believe. We shall examine this problem more carefully in a moment, but real beings from another world in flying saucers (if they are real) could not have any relation to the "make-believe" beings in the Bible.

In regard to the first problem, I cannot prove that flying saucers exist. I can say only that since thousands of people have reported seeing strange objects in the sky, it seems probable that they are seeing something. They may be seeing satellites, stars, or clouds, but they may be seeing much more. But I do not have to be 100 per cent certain that flying saucers exist in order to study the possible relation between the Bible and flying saucers. The Bible reports that the Red Sea parted and enabled the Hebrews to escape from the Egyptians. If I had to be 100 per cent certain that the Red Sea parted *before* I studied the report in the Bible, I might never study the report. But in fact I can study and compare various modern UFO reports and the Biblical UFO reports without having decided ahead of time precisely how accurate or "real" the reports are. Thus, although the uncertain state of the existence of flying saucers has probably delayed a careful theological comparison of modern flying-saucer reports with the Biblical reports of strange objects in the sky, this delay was not an absolute necessity, but rather, a reflection of the generally skeptical temper of our times. Modern theologians have been like swimmers who have assumed that the water was too cold, and have not even bothered to test the temperature with their feet.

But even if flying saucers exist, are they not a modern phenomenon? How could they have anything to do with the Bible? Although the term *flying saucer* is fairly new, and although the UFO "explosion" occurred after World War II, writers such as Donald Keyhoe and Frank Edwards have pointed out that reports of strange objects in the sky have been with us for centuries. UFO writers such as Keyhoe and Edwards suggest that flying saucers may have come to earth in great numbers during and after World War II because of our development of nuclear power. This is not the only suggestion they offer, and I think another factor bears considerable attention.

Marshall McLuhan has spent considerable effort in illustrating the fact that electronic devices such as radio, television, and radar are an extension of man's sensory system —his eyes, ears, and sense of touch. Thus McLuhan speaks about *Understanding Media: The Extensions of Man.*[3]

During World War II we developed air travel and began to build rockets; radar was invented and used, and finally, as the cold war developed, the earth was literally blanketed with electronic sensing devices. As we began to move out into space in our planes, and as people began to look up to see man-made objects in the sky, they also began to see other objects. One really has no idea what sort of fish are in the sea until he baits a hook and drops it into the water. It may be that flying saucers are recent arrivals. Or it may be they have been there all along—for centuries —but that we were more or less unaware of their existence because we only recently developed our sky "fishhooks"— our radar, our planes and rockets, all of which are largely products of World War II. Have flying saucers recently moved into our space, or have we only now moved into their space?

If there is the problem of whether or not flying saucers exist, and if they exist, how long they have inhabited our space, there is also the problem of how *open* modern theology is to discussing an already difficult subject. The difficulty with theology, if it tries to keep up with science, is that there is always a "translation lag" between the development of certain ideas in science and the translation of these same ideas into theological discussion. Thus a man goes to school during the early part of the twentieth century, studies science as it is then, begins writing theology by the 1930s, gains theological stature by the '40s, and finally has his ideas popularized by the '60s, by which time the science on which this theology was based is half a century out of date.

At the beginning of the twentieth century scientists were extremely skeptical about the existence of life anywhere else in the universe. If you apply this thinking to the Biblical material, you might conclude that the beings from another world reported in the Bible had to be mythological—and of course they might be. But now, in the 1960s, most scientists are of the opinion that thousands of other planets in the universe are probably inhabited. That is not to say that all scientists believe in flying saucers, but the fact is that we have moved into the space age; scientific thinking about the universe has changed. But our most "modern" theology—the "death of God" theology—is based on theological assumptions which were in turn based on scientific thinking as it was during the first part of this century. This is what I mean by the "translation lag," and I think that it will be useful to examine briefly some of the current theological statements about the Biblical view of space to illustrate how this "translation lag" has really blinded theology to any serious study of the relation between the Bible and flying saucers.

HONEST TO GOD—IS GOD DEAD?

How does the suggestion that Jesus may have been taken off into space in a flying saucer fit into the context of current theological debate? In fact, this theory does not fit at all. One of the most discussed theological books of the present decade is Bishop John A. T. Robinson's *Honest to God*.[4] This Christian bishop argues that the time has come when no Christian can in "all honesty" believe in certain events which the Bible describes. The Bible has an outdated "make-believe" way of looking at the world; but we in the twentieth century have grown up, and it is time we learned that there is no Santa Claus. On the very first page of the first chapter of his book Robinson says:

> Even such an educated man of the world as St Luke can express the conviction of Christ's ascension—the conviction that he is not merely alive but reigns in the might and right of God—in the crudest terms of being "lifted up" into heaven, there to sit down at the right hand of the Most High. He feels no need to offer any apology for this language, even though he of all New Testament writers was commending Christianity to what Schleiermacher called its "cultured despisers.". . .
>
> Moreover it is the two most mature theologians of the New Testament, St John and the later Paul, who write most uninhibitedly of this "going up" and "coming down." [5]

Now if I understand Robinson correctly, he is suggesting that while St. Luke felt no need "to offer any apology" for the fact that he spoke of the Ascension of Christ in the "crudest terms," Bishop Robinson does feel the need to apologize for Luke's use of this language. According to Robinson, if Luke did not know better than to record the Ascension passage, all thinking men today know better than to try to interpret it realistically, despite the fact that the passage reads like an event anyone could have witnessed.

Why has Robinson mentioned the Ascension of Christ on the first page of his first chapter of *Honest to God*? He might have begun by saying how difficult it is to believe in the Resurrection of Christ, but instead he began with the Ascension. I once heard a theological professor raise the following rhetorical question in his class: "No one today believes in the Ascension, does he?" No one in the

25

class objected to the question or tried to argue in favor of
the Ascension, and in all the "honest to God" debates, I
have read no solid arguments against Bishop Robinson's
opening words regarding the Ascension. Robinson has in
a sense led with an ace; his first card was one he thought
could not be beaten. The question is: Can the concept of
flying saucers in relation to the Ascension trump his ace?
When Bishop Robinson mentioned that Jesus was "lifted
up," he failed to add that the Bible provided a vehicle—
a "cloud"—to do the lifting. It may seem highly unlikely
that Jesus had anything to do with flying saucers, and yet
in the space age we must surely have come to realize that
space travel is not out of the question. Even though a
"cloud" does not seem to offer a very likely space vehicle,
it should receive our serious attention when we are dealing
with something as serious as the Ascension of Christ.

To believe in the bodily Resurrection of Christ, as the
traditional Church has believed, and yet not to believe
in the Ascension, presents difficulties. If we discard the
Ascension, we have to ask: What happened to the resurrected body of Christ? If we do not accept the Bible's
answer to this question—the Ascension—then we have to
make up our own answer. The usual alternative is not to
believe in either the Resurrection or the Ascension. It has
been precisely this type of problem which has led theologians to the idea of the "death of God." The Biblical
material in many ways seems scientifically impossible, and
because of this the Biblical idea of God seems impossible
—God must be dead.

Perhaps no other single factor has contributed more to
current theological skepticism than the problem of trying
to reconcile our scientific understanding of *space* and the

universe with the Biblical view of space and the relation
of the universe to God; it is clear that this problem is behind Robinson's thinking. He says that "we do not realize
how crudely spatial much of the Biblical terminology is" [6]
(by the word *crude* Robinson means roughly *literal*); if,
since the Copernican revolution, some people have been
able to "think of God as in some way 'beyond' outer space,"
at last the situation has caught up with us. "But now it
seems there is no room for him [God], not merely in the
inn, but in the entire universe: for there are no vacant
places left." [7] Robinson admits that he cannot prove that
God is not somewhere beyond space, because there will
always be "gaps" in scientific knowledge. He would undoubtedly say that my flying-saucer theory is simply another "gap" in our knowledge, and when it is solved, we
will finally have to wake up and realize that the "supernatural" events in the Bible are all "myths," stories made
up to suit the occasion.

Science will no longer let us believe in angels, or in
miracles, or in the Ascension of Christ. There are many
scientists today, however, who are convinced that there
may be many superior intelligent beings in our universe,
and a number of scientists have suggested that just as we
are now attempting to travel in space, so other beings from
other worlds may have started traveling in space long ago.
Those who believe in flying saucers believe that we are
being watched by some superior race from another world.
This world view of ours has emerged only over the past
two decades, but at this point it is an interesting coincidence to notice how consistently throughout the development of the Biblical material—which covers a period of
over two thousand years—we find that at the key Biblical

events a person or persons from another world are reported to have been participating, or even causing certain events. We may have reached the point where we now must take this possibility seriously, however unlikely this may seem to the "honest to God" and "death of God" schools of theology. Are angels simply part of our inherited religious mythology, or were superior beings from another world really an important force behind the Biblical religion? Was Jesus one of this group of superior beings, or is this just the impression we get from the childish way of thinking which was part of the mentality of the Biblical authors?

Perhaps one reason Robinson and others of his theological school have not seriously raised this question is that the theologians who prepared the background for Robinson's work did their thinking before the space age, and here I have in mind Rudolf Bultmann, Dietrich Bonhoeffer, and Paul Tillich. While Robinson seems to derive his philosophy from Tillich and his ethics from Bonhoeffer, his opening comments on the Ascension of Christ and the Biblical view of space reflect the type of thought which has been most clearly developed by Bultmann. It is Bultmann who has given us the word *demythologize*, which means to recognize the supernatural events described in the Bible (e.g., the Ascension of Christ) as mythological rather than historical; we must then proceed to reinterpret such myth in terms modern man can understand. Bultmann has chosen "existential" philosophy as the mold in which the demythologized Bible is to be reshaped. For Bultmann, demythologizing is the modern theological miracle by which water is changed into wine. A childish way of thinking is fermented through existentialism.

What is demythologizing? There are almost as many

answers to this question as there are theologians who write about it, but all demythologizers seem to agree on one basic premise: Many of the traditions recorded in the Bible appear, on the surface, to represent historical facts, or at least some fundamental facts with various interpretations added. But many of these "facts" are scientifically impossible; in a sense, they are simply symbolic representations of the "inner emotions" of man—an attempt to externalize man's psychological experiences.

A young boy came home from Sunday school, and his mother inquired as to what he had learned. The boy explained that the teacher had given a lesson on Moses and the parting of the Red Sea. The mother asked, "What did the teacher say about Moses?" The boy replied, "Well, the Egyptian army chased the Israelites to the Red Sea, and then Moses called up the Marines and they built a pontoon bridge across the sea and the Israelites crossed on the bridge with the Egyptians coming right behind them. When the Israelites had safely crossed, Moses ordered the bridge to be dynamited, and the army of Egypt was drowned in the sea." The mother pursued the matter further; she asked, "Is that really what your teacher said?" "No," the boy admitted with hesitation, "but if I told it the way she told it, you would never believe it." We shall be examining the Red Sea incident more closely in a later chapter, but all of us can undoubtedly share the boy's tension in trying to make sense of the Red Sea story. Some modern theologians have tried to come to grips with this type of Biblical problem by demythologizing it—by stressing aspects of the story that came from man's imagination rather than from history.

Demythologizing seems to be carried out by degrees,

depending on one's scientifically or Biblically informed skepticism. Thus while Bishop Robinson accepts many of the implications of Bultmann's work, as in regard to the Ascension of Christ, Robinson criticizes Bultmann for being part of a kind of "scientific dogmatism" and for being too skeptical concerning the reports of the Resurrection of Christ. Demythologizers are by no means in agreement as to what ought and what ought not to be allowed as Biblical fact, and what must be called myth.[8] There is quite a spectrum even within the demythologizing camp, but the common ground of this approach to the Bible is the assumption that many of the reports in the Bible that appear to be factual or "realistic" are in fact myth.

We have to admit immediately that there is much historical evidence to support the view that much of the Biblical material is mythological. Bultmann has paid particular attention to ancient mystery religions which are clearly mythological and has used this foundation to predict similar patterns in Christianity. Certainly much of the Biblical language is symbolic—although in a sense all language is symbolic—but I would not want every word in the Bible translated literally, although the "symbol" may point to a reality which is literally real. The Bible reports that Jesus was crucified. I know of no theologian who has argued that the Biblical report of the Crucifixion is "mythological." Everyone seems to agree that Jesus really— literally—was crucified. But when we read that Thomas sought to touch the wounds in the hands of the risen Christ, our scientific imagination is stretched, and we then suggest that this report has a mythological origin.

How can we tell the difference between Biblical fact

and fancy? This is the question. At the risk of pointing to the obvious, there are roughly two camps within the Christian Church, which are usually called *conservative* and *liberal*. In our own age, the conservatives try to interpret the Bible "realistically," whereas the liberals are more concerned with "demythologizing." The Church is composed of a spectrum of beliefs, ranging from extreme "realistic" Biblical interpretation, which turns the Bible into something like a dictionary or machine producing salvation, to the extreme "demythologized" interpretation, in which the main value of the Bible is its "literary" form rather than its historical content. But most of the time both groups are aiming at what they hope is the "true" meaning or significance of the Biblical material.

The suggestion that Jesus was taken away from earth in a flying saucer (or something like one) is obviously a "realistic" interpretation of the Biblical material. But it is not a literal interpretation of the Biblical material, for the Bible says that he was taken away in a "cloud." For this reason I prefer the term *realistic* to *literal* as a means of explaining my approach to Biblical exegesis. I am concerned about the truth. If it is *true* that the disciples really did see Jesus lifted up before their eyes in a "cloud," then to demythologize this report is a mistake of a very high order. If it is true that flying saucers really exist, it is a mistake to ignore or cover up the fact of their existence. But Truth is an extremely difficult prize to capture. I cannot be certain that there is no truth in demythologizing. I can certainly see how Bultmann and Robinson have been led to their present positions. The problem of the Biblical view of space is painfully difficult.

31

Bultmann has done the most to make us aware of this difficulty. In his work *Jesus Christ and Mythology* Bultmann explains part of the basis of demythologizing:

> For the world-view of the Scripture is mythological and is therefore unacceptable to modern man whose thinking has been shaped by science and is therefore no longer mythological. Modern man always makes use of technical means which are the result of science. . . . Have you read anywhere in them [the newspapers] that political or social or economic events are performed by supernatural powers such as God, angels or demons? [9]

One reason the concept of demythologizing presents such a problem is that there is a considerable amount of truth in it. Not even the most conservative theologian would argue that our "world view" today is the same as the world view of men two thousand years ago. In a society of planned obsolescence, synthetic drugs, and teen-age fads it is impossible to believe that man's world is static. Yet there are activities common to man today and two thousand years ago that hardly need to be interpreted for our own times. On one occasion we read in Scripture (John 21:9 ff.) that Jesus apparently built a charcoal fire and prepared fish for the disciples to eat after they came in from their fishing boat. Jesus offered them breakfast of fish and bread. There seems to be nothing here that offends the modern mind, that needs to be "demythologized," except for the fact that the Bible maintains that the occasion on which Jesus prepared this breakfast "was now the third time that Jesus was revealed to the disciples after he was raised from the dead" (John 21:14).

Bishop Robinson explains the case for demythologizing the New Testament by saying that just as we had the great debate over a "literal" creation a century ago, now the debate must be over "the last things."

> Is it necessary for the Biblical faith to be expressed in terms of this world-view, which in its way is as primitive philosophically as the Genesis stories are primitive scientifically? [10]

Robinson's mistake here is similar to the mistake fundamentalists seem to make: the fact that the Bible is a single book under one cover helps us to forget that the Biblical material was collected over a period of time which is about equal to the time that lies between us and the life of Christ. If Christians a century ago made the mistake of trying to defend the Creation story as an account which in its own way was as scientific and historical as the Biblical description of the Crucifixion of Christ, so now "demythologizers" are assuming that since Genesis had to be demythologized, everything must be so treated. There is a world of difference between Genesis 1, Psalms, Matthew, Acts, and Revelation.

One rule by which we might approach the problem of deciding whether it may be dangerous to demythologize a particular passage in Scripture is to investigate on one hand to what extent the materials involved seem to represent an interpretation of a particular experience, and on the other hand what materials comprise *description,* or reporting of empirical data. Interpretation and description are of course tightly interwoven, and yet even the most devoted demythologizer will usually admit that there was a historical Jesus of some sort. It seems fair to assume that the disciples shared common experiences with this Jesus —such as eating a meal with him. The total sum of their experiences led the disciples to the interpretation (with the prompting of the Holy Spirit) that Jesus was the Christ. But what sort of experiences brought the disciples to the conclusion that Jesus was the Christ? Why did the disciples settle on him as the Christ rather than on one of the two thieves crucified with him?

Those who consider the Resurrection of Christ "mythological" must suppose that the Resurrection was an idea which the disciples projected onto Jesus. "Resurrections" were part of the mythological world view of the Bible. But the Biblical materials lead us to believe that it was no more part of the Biblical world view for people to rise from the dead than it is part of our world view. The Gospel of John even records that the hardheaded empiricist Thomas said, "Unless I see in his hands the print of the nails, and place my finger in the mark of the nails, and place my hand in his side, I will not believe" (John 20:25). If the Resurrection is mythological, then this passage is meant deliberately to deceive us. The Resurrection seems to be something we all could have experienced if we had been there—but we were not, and therefore we suspect that it should be demythologized.

Bishop Robinson asks: "Is it necessary for the Biblical faith to be expressed in terms of this world-view?" this "primitive" world view. Cannot we reinterpret the Biblical materials without losing anything? It seems to me that if we demythologize the Resurrection, we have little right as a Church to preach that the "existential resurrection" of Christ will ensure Christians eternal life—life after death. It may be selfish to be concerned with life after death, but Jesus treats life after death as a "fact"—it happens to people. If it is a fact, for the Church to "demythologize" this fact will undoubtedly be a great disservice to the human race—and to the gospel itself. The gospel seems to offer eternal resurrected life to Christians. What God has given is not the domain of theology to take away. Jesus believed in a world of resurrected persons and of angels. They go together. Although the idea of angels may be an offense to our modern minds, perhaps we can endure the offense for the sake of the "profit" motive.

In any case, we have arrived at the point where we have to take seriously again the idea that perhaps intelligent superior beings were at work bringing about the Biblical religion. These beings were not totally responsible for the Biblical religion—the religion grew among men, in the midst of flesh, blood, and history. But who planted the religion? Did man deceive himself; did he create God himself, in his own image? Or, as the Bible suggests, did God create man in his image? The Bible suggests, as we shall shortly see in detail, that God made himself known through "angels," beings from another world. I have said almost nothing up to this point about God, whether with Bishop Robinson he is "up there" or "out there" or wherever. Nor have I said much about God's being dead, with Thomas J. J. Altizer.[11] Jesus said, "He who has seen me has seen the Father" (John 14:9). If God was in Christ, then it has only to be shown that there are good grounds for believing that Jesus is now alive, and it will also have been shown that God is no more dead now than he ever was. Was Christ raised from the dead? Did he ascend before the disciples to another world? These are the questions.

The Bible clearly claims in many key instances that "Unidentified Flying Objects" played a significant role in the development of the Hebrew-Christian faith, and it also claims that superior beings from another world (angels) made significant contributions at various times. The question I am here raising is: What is the evidence for a "realistic" rather than a "mythological" interpretation of the relevant Biblical and modern data, and what is its significance?

INTELLECTUAL HONESTY AND THE PROBABILITY OF TRUTH

There is one other subsidiary aspect of the current theological debate to which I wish to draw attention. Those who are trying to remove the supernatural aspects of the Christian faith by demythologizing or some other process usually do so in the name of "intellectual honesty." Thus Bishop Robinson has given his book the title *Honest to God;* he believes that the strength of his position lies in his intellectual honesty. Bishop James Pike, who seems to share Robinson's basic sentiments, has written a book entitled *A Time for Christian Candor.*[12] Bultmann, who has led the demythologizing program, speaks about a "sacrificium intellectus." [13] Whether the expression is in Latin or English, whether the word is *honesty* or *candor,* the basic implication is the same. It is intellectually dishonest for Christians to continue to support the orthodox Christian interpretation of the Biblical materials which are apparently supernatural, such as the Resurrection and the Ascension. Robinson explains, "All I can do is to try to be honest —honest to God and about God—and to follow the argument wherever it leads." [14]

Now I certainly do not recommend that theologians be

dishonest. Yet I do not believe that honesty should be the only test, or the primary test, of the adequacy of any theology. One of the main reasons modern theologians argue the need to be "honest" about theology is that our "modern scientific world view" will no longer allow us to accept a realistic Christian faith. I believe it is interesting that Albert Einstein never wrote a book under the title *Honest to Relativity* or *A Time for Scientific Candor.* Scientists generally do not concern themselves with honesty in their books. They are interested in something else—*truth.* When people read a book by a scientist, they assume that he is being honest, and they also assume that the main aim of a scientist's book is to try to get at the truth, however elusive truth may be.

If we are concerned about the "scientific world view," we would do well to follow the example of scientists and keep *truth* rather than *honesty* as the major goal of our theological studies; if we do not, we can easily fall into a pit. A blind man may with all honesty maintain that light does not exist; men who can see light will perhaps commend the honesty of the blind man, but they will wish that he were more concerned with the truth about the existence of light. He might, through careful research, discover his blindness as the cause of the fact that he does not believe in the existence of light. I am not suggesting that theologians such as Robinson are blind; this book may have less truth in it than Robinson's *Honest to God.* Robinson is a well-trained theologian. But I do not believe that, in saying, "All I can do is to try to be honest," Robinson is in fact being honest. Cannot Robinson try to be truthful—even if he fails? In fact, does not Robinson suppose that his book approaches more than honesty—that it approaches the truth? It is much easier to be satisfied with achieving honesty than truth, although in this age—which is all too well aware of the subconscious desires of Freudian psychology—I think that we would all be suspect of how capable any of us are of truly being honest. Furthermore, if any of us asks the question of ourselves, "Am I truly being honest in my religious beliefs?" we would all have to answer, "I am not certain," and in all probability we would be left with guilt feelings about our religious honesty. This type of thinking does a lot of unnecessary damage to the Christian Church; if liberal theologians who raise the question of "honesty" wonder why conservatives often react with hostility toward them, I think that one cause is right here. All Christians have enough guilt feelings with which to deal without the added burden of feeling guilty about being a Christian.

If we focus upon the problem of truth rather than the concept of honesty, we shall find that this problem of guilt disappears. Of course, it may be difficult to believe a realistic interpretation of the Christian religion—that Jesus turned water to wine or rose from the dead—but if a person is convinced that the realistic interpretation is true, however improbable, it would seem that he can believe it if he so desires (without feeling guilty). It is probably more than coincidental that Bultmann recommends that after the Christian faith is demythologized, the faith then be expressed in terms of "existential" philosophy. Sigmar von Fersen opens his definition of "Existential Philosophy" by saying that it "determines the worth of knowledge not in relation to truth but according to its biological value contained in the pure data of consciousness." [15] I think that the influence of existential philosophy on theology helps account for the fact that many theologians such as Robinson are concerned with "honesty" rather than with "truth."

Jesus said that he was the truth (John 14:6), and Paul encouraged Christians to think about "whatsoever things are true" (Philippians 4:8). While a study of the Biblical idea of truth might be useful, most of us undoubtedly share Pilate's confusion, "What is truth?" (John 18:38). Pilate's mistake was not in raising the question, but in washing his hands of the question in the face of a difficult situation.

In the field of science men often find it useful to deal with truth within limits. In a hypothetical situation, let us say, the purity of a chemical must range between 80 and 90 per cent. A quality control technician will find the chemical suitably "true" if it lies somewhere in the range of 85 per cent plus or minus 5 per cent. The purity of this chemical may vary with certain degrees, and the probability of the success of any experiment using this chemical depends on the success of the quality control person. Einstein's theory of relativity has made us more conscious of the extent to which the observer himself limits the adequacy of any theory or experiment. Every scientist is limited by the scientific age in which he lives. Isaac Newton made a fantastic contribution to the fields of dynamics and optics, but he did not have an electron microscope or knowledge of nuclear physics to see that his idea of a "solid" atom was not true. In the face of the evidence at his disposal, he suggested that atoms were hard and unbreakable, but that was in the seventeenth century. Bultmann recognizes, at least verbally, that "The science of today is no longer the same as it was in the nineteenth century, and to be sure, all the results of science are relative, and no world-view of yesterday or today or tomorrow is definitive." [16] Thus, if our world view is constantly changing, why should science force us to demythologize? Because what science has really given us is not so much concrete explanations but a way of thinking about the world, science attempts "to give reasonable proofs for every statement." [17] The contrast between the Biblical and modern world view is between two types of thinking, the mythological (Biblical) and the scientific (which requires proofs). Here again we cannot help noticing doubting Thomas. If the Bible is unconcerned with "proof," the whole sequence in which Thomas seeks to touch the risen Christ is out of place with the "mythological" way of thinking. We shall return to the problem of "proof" in religion and science later, but I shall simply point out that it is *possible* that the disciples followed Christ, and proclaimed his Resurrection, because they had no choice. For them it was a historical fact, or certainly it could have been.

If Christ would appear to us all, the problem would be solved. But the evidence behind the Biblical faith varies within limits or degrees. Thomas and the Apostle Paul were subjected to the highest degree of empirical verification. Those who talked immediately to the disciples also had a reasonably high degree of verification, especially when the disciples worked miracles. We have the written Biblical record, but when one accepts the premise that the Biblical material is "mythological," this of course weakens any possible witness of the Bible from a realistic point of view. Those who decide in favor of a realistic Biblical interpretation will undoubtedly share the emotional temper of Thomas. Perhaps if persons were subjected to higher degrees of verification they would make more effective

Christians, and it may be that one reason only God can judge in the last day (Matthew 7:1) is that only he knows the extent to which each man has been subjected to the claims of the gospel—the degree of verification which has sought to claim him for Christ, especially the informing presence of the Holy Spirit.

If both science and theology, however, are only relatively true, or true within certain limits, why should we be concerned about the accuracy of one theology over another, or one church over another? Why are not all religious beliefs equally valid? In science if the quality control of a chemical does not keep it within the prescribed limits—between 80 and 90 per cent pure—it may cease to function. If a chemical does not measure up to minimum specifications, it may be useless for industrial purposes. Theologians attempt to maintain the purity or truth of their research within certain limits—although these limits may be relative rather than absolute, because it seems likely that the further from the "norm" Christian theology deviates, the less effective it is. If theologians pay no attention to the quality control aspect of their work, they may cease to be Christian theologians. The Bible, or creeds such as the Apostles' Creed, are yardsticks or standards by which we test the purity of any theology. But theology is a human enterprise, and no one theologian can be dogmatic about his own work. He can point to the evidence and compare it with the "standards," but with humility he must realize the limits of his own vision. Theology, like science, is both an individual and a community affair. Orthodoxy or the "scientific consensus of opinion" is a vector which results from the tension between the liberal and the conservative Christian. Between the liberal and the conservative there is a whole spectrum of belief, the total sum of which represents the Church.

If this is the approach of both science and theology to the problem of truth, what can Bishop Robinson mean by intellectual dishonesty? It might be that there are still people on earth who do not believe that man shall someday safely reach the moon. This is not my own belief, however, and I believe that the evidence suggests that we shall soon place a man on the moon. It is quite probable that we shall reach the moon by 1970, and even more probable that we shall reach it by 1980. Is any person intellectually dishonest who now doubts that we shall ever reach the moon? Not necessarily. A third world war, or some scientific barrier yet unseen, might make the trip impossible, so that it is by no means yet proved that we shall reach the moon. Suppose, however, that we do place a man on the moon by 1970, and suppose that in 1971 there are still well-informed people who do not believe that we shall ever succeed in placing a man on the moon. We would say not only that these persons are intellectually dishonest, but that they may well have some psychological disorder. They cannot distinguish between truth and falsehood. I think Bishop Robinson is arguing (although he does not say so in these words) that the evidence in regard to the Ascension of Christ is so clear that those who continue to include the Ascension among their beliefs are doing so against the facts. But the existence of flying saucers could very well throw Robinson's "facts" into grave doubt. Just as we have not yet reached the moon, I do not believe that we have reached the point where we can announce to the world that the Ascension did not happen as it is recorded in Acts 1.

While I have generally been arguing in favor of belief in the Ascension, I must point out that there is value in doubting it. Robinson may be doing the Church a considerable service by doubting the Ascension, in a roundabout way. If a person cannot doubt, he cannot be a Christian any more than he can be a Christian if he cannot believe. The Middle Ages suffered from corruption and superstition largely because people were too gullible. Doubt works as a tremendous purifying force, although, carried to an extreme, as with the philosophy of René Descartes (who even doubted his own existence), doubt can lead to a blind alley. But if a person cannot doubt, he may be led to believe in many false theologies and false Christs (Matthew 24:24).

Bishop Robinson has a right to doubt a realistic interpretation of the Ascension of Christ. Michael Polanyi, in his *Personal Knowledge*, has shown that scientific truth emerges in the tension between the belief of a scientist in a particular theory and the doubt of another scientist about it.[18] The truth about the Ascension will be arrived at only by the exercise of our ability to seek, doubt, and believe.

Thus in this book we shall be concerned about whether or not flying saucers exist, how long they have been with us, and what possible relation flying saucers may have to the Bible. But we are concerned with other things as well: the way in which our hypothesis concerning the Bible and flying saucers fits into current theological debate, and to some extent the problem of scientific method and the problem of truth. If we keep these problems in mind, we can partially understand why even the suggestion of a relation between the Bible and flying saucers seems ridiculous—which it may be. Finally, we shall be concerned with any possible relation between the Bible and modern views of the structure of space, as suggested by Einstein's theory of relativity. Does the idea of the "curvature" of space have any bearing on the Biblical idea of "heaven"? In this book we are going to explore the Bible and the space age. We do not know how "true" the various hypotheses we are presenting may prove to be. But it is our impression that the relation between the Biblical view of space and our modern scientific view of space is by no means settled. A demythologized theology has confined Biblical studies to the surface of a sphere—earth. But now we have moved up, into the third dimension; and science has even moved into the "fourth dimension." I believe that the situation is extremely open; I see very little in modern science which excludes most of the Biblical beliefs about space. The space age has set us free to explore the Bible in a new way.

CHAPTER II

WHAT IS THE PROBABILITY THAT FLYING SAUCERS EXIST?

The degree of probability of my hypothesis depends on (1) the probability of the existence of flying saucers (which transport beings from another world to ours) and (2) the probability that these space vehicles are the same ones the Bible describes as having been pivotal in the development of the Biblical religion.

Do flying saucers exist? We must keep in mind with Michael Polanyi that this is both a personal and a factual question. A person becomes a "believer" in UFOs on the basis of a certain amount of evidence which convinces him that he must choose to believe rather than doubt. A person who doubts that UFOs exist might be a person who almost always doubts everything; such a person might have been heard saying fifteen years ago, "We will never send a man to the moon." He may still be saying so today. On the other hand, the "believer" may be a very gullible person —he may believe in astrology (which I do not), or at a very advanced age he may still believe in Santa Claus. Some persons are more open to belief; others, to doubt. Some people are extremely skeptical about some things, while simultaneously being gullible about others. The "degree of probability" which I emotionally feel about the existence of UFOs is 70 per cent belief and 30 per cent doubt, or something on that order. What I believe, however, does not alter the facts: saucers either exist or do not exist. Modern weather information sometimes suggests that there is a "10 per cent probability of rain or snow"; probably it will not rain—but then it might. I am suggesting here the degree of probability that Jesus ascended into space in a UFO which looked like a modern flying saucer.

Part of the reason it will be difficult for the average person to believe that Jesus ascended into space in some sort of vehicle is that very few people today understand or accept the Biblical view of angels. What is clear throughout the Biblical material, however, is that God's will for the Jews, and eventually for all mankind, was "revealed" by beings from another world. Usually these beings looked very much like ordinary human beings (they almost never have wings); God made man "for a little while lower than the angels" (Hebrews 2:7), a "little while" because eventually men become angels, or like angels, in the resurrection world (Matthew 22:30). It was to the resurrection world, the world of angels, that Christ returned at the Ascension (Acts 1:9). Two men from another world were present at the scene of the Ascension to explain to the disciples the significance of what they had just witnessed (Acts 1:10, 11). Few can read the Bible without getting the distinct impression that the Biblical religion—in both the Old and the New Testaments—was a religion which was delivered to a select group of people by beings from another world. Once the "package" of the Biblical religion had been delivered, man became responsible for the distribution of the contents of the package.

When I say that the "package" of the Biblical religion was delivered, I do not mean to imply that the Bible is that package. The Biblical people "digested" the contents of the package, much as John "ate" the heavenly scroll (Revelation 10:10). The Bible contains witnessed and digested revelation, but it is important to remember that not everything recorded in the Bible was a revelation from beings from another world. The Bible also records family history, wars, rulers, and church history. But the heart of the Biblical religion was a "package" from heaven, finally embodied in Jesus himself. The Greek word for *angel* means a *messenger;* thus the word *angel* is an essentially functional description. A person who preached the gospel was called an *evangelist,* and the Greek word, like the English word, contains the word *angel*—ev-angel-ist. The disciples themselves became "angels" in the sense that they became messengers, preaching Christ in strange worlds. Christ was the package, and the elements of bread and wine were distributed by the "evangelists" as the Eucharist. At the Ascension the parting instructions of Christ to his disciples were to preach the gospel in all the world (Acts 1:8). They had been given the riches of the gospel, and they became the stewards of the gospel. Just as Amer-

47

ica with her riches has responded to a starving world by sending Care packages, so the disciples were commissioned to take their riches, the bread of heaven, and distribute it in a spiritually poor world. Jesus had three words for Peter: "Feed my sheep" (John 21:17).

Thus the question of whether or not flying saucers exist is not merely a question of whether we are being visited by beings from another world. It is possible that these beings who are watching us are the very same beings who stimulated the Biblical religion. Jesus gave the impression that the "angels" are very much concerned about the success of the gospel on earth; he went so far as to say that "there is joy before the angels of God over one sinner who repents" (Luke 15:10). Angels seem to be emotionally as well as actively involved in the success or failure of the gospel. One may very well wonder, if these angels are so concerned about the success of the gospel, why they do not take a more obviously active part in "evangelism." If a UFO landed on the White House lawn, and a being from another world emerged and proceeded to make a worldwide television broadcast urging people to accept the Biblical religion, perhaps several conversions would follow. But if we are now being watched by beings from another world—the same beings who initiated the Biblical religion—then it seems clear that they are following a general *laissez-faire* policy. The gospel aims to have men become "children of God" (John 1:12), that is, mature, responsible sons. It could certainly be argued that since Biblical times we have been weaned from the milk on which the Church began—we have had to survive on strong meat in the past few centuries, not without problems of indigestion. We have been allowed to wage our wars and build our concentration camps; we have had to sink or swim in world affairs.

In the twelfth chapter of the book of Acts we read that Herod placed Peter in prison, and the night before Peter was to have been killed, an angel came and let Peter out of prison. Because he was asleep when the angel arrived, Peter thought that the whole sequence was a dream, but the angel led him out into the street and then departed from him. Peter was still dazed, but he decided that he might as well walk "to the house of Mary," and Luke suggests that a girl by the name of Rhoda was so shocked to hear Peter's voice that she forgot to open the door. One significant fact about this passage is that the angel did not linger. He came, did his job, and left immediately. He did not go with Peter and stay for a midnight snack. One does not get the impression on reading the Bible that one could go into any coffee shop on main street in Jerusalem and find an angel. If a situation was really desperate, an angel might move in to save it. But as soon as his job was finished, he got out of the way of the Church. Angels did not usually interfere. They did not save Stephen, and apparently Peter was martyred later at Rome. The main point at this time is that if we are being watched rather than contacted by beings from another world who initiated the Biblical religion, it appears consistent with their policy of remaining aloof from our historical situation whenever possible.

Angels in History

There have been essentially two ideas of angels which have dominated Western thinking—the Biblical and the

Greek. While some Greek angels bore resemblance to human beings, the Greeks also developed the concept of the soul which was in many ways similar to a geometric point. One gets the impression in Plato's *Timaeus* and Aristotle's *Physica* that the human soul is analogous to a geometric point and that it is from the concept of the point that geometry is derived—geometry representing an uncontaminated form of pure thought.[1] Centuries later this concept of the geometric point-soul serves as a similar basis for the monads of Leibniz. The Greeks believed that the human soul had its origin in the point-stars on the outer sphere of the universe, and at death the human soul escaped from its body to return to the geometric-soul-point-star in space from which it had originally come. Astrology arose directly from this world view. Angels that were like points were therefore basically invisible, and the Greeks often used these angels as an explanation of the invisible "cause" behind events. Before the discovery of the laws of momentum, an angel might cause a stone to fall or the sun to go around the earth.

In the Bible, however, angels are essentially humanlike beings that have come from "above," from another world out in space. They are not usually invisible, although the sequence with Balaam's ass (Numbers 22:21 ff.) may be an exception. The Bible, particularly the New Testament, develops the concept of the resurrection of the body, in which men become like angels, in direct contrast to the Greek view in which only man's soul is saved (and his body lost). The Biblical world view presents such a problem in the face of modern science because it stresses the resurrection of the body—and presumably bodies must occupy some place in space. Where? If we were committed to the Greek view of salvation, then we could say that eternal life is merely a "state" since a point-soul has essentially no spatial properties, or at least spatial dimensions.

As the gospel was preached in the Greek world, the two divergent views of angels and salvation were mixed in the evolution of Christian doctrine. By the time we reach Thomas Aquinas in the mid-thirteenth century, we find that Aquinas in the "Treatise on Angels" in his *Summa Theologica* can wonder about the size of angels in comparison with a pin.[2] The answer depends on whether one is thinking of Biblical or Greek angels. Aquinas defined angels as pure "soul" beings, without the bodies of men. In the Bible we do not find that the basic difference between man and angels is that man has a body; both have bodies. The difference is that man is from earth; angels come from another world.

When Copernicus and Galileo shattered the celestial spheres of Ptolemy, the eschatology of Aquinas and of the Christian Church as a whole suffered. The Reformation attempted with some success to separate Biblical theology from Greek philosophy, and there was some revival of a Biblical view of angels. Isaac Newton, who devoted at least as much time to his Protestant theology as he did to his science, was thoroughly committed to a belief in Biblical angels, in the resurrection of the body, and in a "heaven" somewhere in outer space. He was, in both his science and his theology, thoroughly against "vain philosophy," as he called it; that is, he was against Aristotle.

As the scientific revolution continued, however, and the age of Darwinian evolution emerged, it no longer seemed possible for a scientist to be committed to the Biblical world view. The concept of evolution, together with the science of genetics, was based in part on the idea of "chance," and as scientists surveyed man's environment, they concluded that it was by pure chance, a freak accident of the universe, that man ever appeared. When all the atmospheric conditions, temperature conditions, gravitational forces, rotation rate of the earth—to name a few of the factors involved in sustaining life—were considered, it seemed that the earth was probably the only place in the universe with life. Man was alone in a vast, impersonal machine. Like a little boy lost in a wood, we began to whistle a "happy" tune to pretend that we were not afraid. Men of science and literature began asking man to grow up and face his destiny. Out of this mentality arose the idea of progress and the social gospel. We are asked to "demythologize" the primitive Biblical religion; we must mature; we must grow up.

But as the twentieth century continued, so did scientific advance. During World War II we moved into the air with our planes and with radar; the Germans developed the principle of the rocket, and with the war past, the space age began. As we moved into space with rockets, planes, radar, and radio telescopes, our world view began to change. We began to think seriously again about a universe with many inhabitants, and we began looking for life from other worlds. We were no longer confined in our thinking to our two-dimensional demythologized earth. We broke through the space barrier; we became aware again of our three-dimensional universe. Was there life on Mars or Venus? Science fiction came forth with all sorts of imaginative answers, but even a measured scientific view based again on "chance" or probability suggested that because of the vast size of our universe, there may be millions of inhabited planets even within our own Milky Way. Many well-informed scientists began to suspect that other races might have evolved in the course of time, and that long ago other beings might have attempted to travel in space—perhaps even to our earth.

At the end of World War II, as we moved into space, we began to see "Unidentified Flying Objects," objects which many thought were space vehicles from another world which were watching us. Bishop Robinson's *Honest to God* is based on Rudolf Bultmann's demythologizing principles, which were in turn based on the science Bultmann learned at the beginning of the twentieth century, before the space age began. Is it possible that Robinson's *Honest to God* is based on scientific thinking which is now out of date?

Not only has "demythologizing" kept us from thinking seriously about angels, but also we have not thoroughly separated the Biblical from the Greek view of angels. Scientific method seeks to explain reality in terms of the testable, and the Greek "invisible" soul-point angels are untestable. As J. Bronowski has said in *The Common Sense of Science*,

> As much as bookkeeping, government and doing the weekend shopping, science is an activity of putting order into our experience. So much was true even of the science of Aquinas. To this was added in the sixteenth and seventeenth centuries a new assumption about the kind of order which science sets out to find or make. Roughly, the assumption amounts to this, that science is to get rid of angels, blue fairies with red noses, and other agents whose intervention would reduce the explanation of physical events to other than physical terms. The world is regular in itself; the world is a machine.[3]

In a certain sense I agree with Bronowski that the task of science is to get rid of angels or "blue fairies" as explanations of natural phenomena. Thus I do not believe that angels keep the earth turning on its axis; I believe that the earth's momentum keeps it rotating. Science seeks to find the *cause* for the visible *effect*. Bronowski does not consider angels a legitimate cause; but we have to ask, What is the cause of the Biblical religion? We know the effect. It is recorded in Scriptures. The demythologizers would say that the basic cause behind the Biblical religion is psychological; it is a religion man has synthesized because of certain inner needs. But the Scriptures give as their own cause the suggestion that beings from another world—angels—were the external agent which caused the Hebrew-Christian tradition. In the space age I do not think we are compelled to believe that this explanation is necessarily mythological, although of course it could be. To give a human analogy, I should think that if some of our astronauts were sent to another planet, and they were to discover a primitive people, and if these astronauts were specifically instructed to lead these people to a particular religious commitment, they might very well succeed. These primitive people might record the fact that beings from another world caused the birth of their religion. In this instance I would request that Bronowski make an exception to his general rule of not admitting angels into his scientific explanation of things, for to exclude angels would be to exclude at least the clue to the correct explanation. I would also ask theological demythologizers to be more willing to admit that the original source of religious beliefs may have been external to man's psyche.

One might well argue that it is scientifically improbable

that such a sequence of events would take place, but I cannot think of grounds on which such an explanation is automatically scientifically out of the question, providing that we separate the Biblical from the Greek way of thinking about angels. It is on these grounds that I think Bishop Robinson is wrong in suggesting that it is *dishonest* for Christians to go on believing in the Ascension of Christ. Bishop Robinson has the right to maintain that the Ascension is highly improbable, but it is by no means impossible in the light of present scientific thinking, particularly if one provides Christ with an adequate space vehicle. One may not be pleased with the theological implications of the suggestion that Christ ascended in some sort of space vehicle; but the implications fit the evidence better than the suggestion that there was no Ascension at all.

If flying saucers exist, if they are in fact space vehicles from another world, and if they have the performance capabilities described in various UFO reports, then there is no doubt that these vehicles would have provided adequate transportation for any beings who might have been involved in nourishing the Biblical religion. We have become aware of these UFOs only since our move into space during and after World War II. If we had not moved into space, perhaps we would not have noticed them even yet. At present these UFOs seem to be interested mainly in surveillance, not in making contact. Who can say that these beings have not been maintaining surveillance for the past four thousand years? The possibility stretches the imagination, but it cannot be ruled out *a priori*. Furthermore, we cannot be sure that there are not several groups of beings, perhaps from many different worlds, watching us, as we might watch fish in a pond.

THE UFO CONTROVERSY

The whole question of the existence of UFOs will not be settled until the U.S. Air Force makes all its space surveillance facilities available to some independent organization for a thorough investigation. A recent newspaper article, headlined "Air Force Plans 'Flying Saucers' Probe," said that "the Air Force is trying to get a leading university to investigate some episodes in depth." The reason for the investigation is that there have been "widespread charges that the Air Force was concealing the truth lest there be a panic." [4] The Government has since "hired the University of Colorado, whose Dr. Edward U. Condon will direct a study project which will involve more than 100 scientists down here to determine who's up there. The idea behind all this is to get the Air Force off the spot and convince the public that earthlings are in no great danger from what are officially known as UFOs," according to the New York *Daily News*.[5]

Who has been charging that members of the Air Force have concealed the truth? A number of persons have led the assault, but certainly one of the first, Major Donald E. Keyhoe, who has written a number of well-documented books, including *Flying Saucers from Outer Space, Flying Saucers Are Real, The Flying Saucer Conspiracy*, and *Flying Saucers: Top Secret*. Keyhoe has also headed the National Investigations Committee on Aerial Phenomena which has compiled the work *The UFO Evidence*. In *The Flying Saucer Conspiracy*, published in 1955, Keyhoe outlined the program of a "conspiracy" of silence on the part of the U.S. Air Force personnel to keep UFO information from the public. Other books, such as *Anatomy of a Phenomenon* by Jacques Vallee and *Report on Unidentified Flying Objects* by Captain Edward Ruppelt, together with the recent *Flying Saucers—Serious Business* by Frank Edwards, have tended to support Keyhoe's thesis that members of the Air Force have concealed evidence concerning UFOs from the public. Most UFO authors are convinced that flying saucers either contain beings from another world or that they are remote-controlled spaceships from another planet. But there seems to be no consensus as to what the beings may look like or where they may have come from, although speculation of course abounds. I am not going to attempt a detailed summary of the various UFO books, but I shall bring out some points which are important for Biblical studies.

According to Keyhoe, Air Force pilots are under restrictions not to give out information to the public concerning UFO contacts. I wrote to the Air Force concerning the UFO situation and received in the mail what was described as "The current report on Project Blue Book," which dealt with material up to 1965. In this report the following comment appears: "The Air Force does not deny the possibility that some form of life may exist on other planets in the universe. However, to date, the Air Force has neither received nor discovered any evidence which proves the existence of intra-space mobility of extraterrestrial life." The following paragraph adds, however, "Anyone observing what he considers to be an unidentified flying object should report it to the nearest Air Force Base." [6] The Air Force position seems clear. They deny having "proof" that UFOs from another world exist. I have already discussed the nature of scientific "proof" in terms of what may be called "probability," and no scientist ever claims that he has absolute "proof" of anything. He may, however, have very convincing evidence. I cannot help wondering if, while the Air Force does not have "proof," it may in fact have considerable evidence that UFOs from another world exist. Furthermore, I cannot help wondering why members of the Air Force are anxious to carry on their UFO program if they have "no evidence." The report encourages the individual to report UFO sightings to the nearest Air Force base. "Project Blue Book" began eighteen years ago. If members of the Air Force really believe that UFOs do not exist, why after eighteen years do they still want sightings to be reported?

The Air Force report also included the indication of some of the restrictions concerning UFOs. "The following items are for internal use only and are *not* available for distribution to the public. These concern internal management and procedures for forwarding UFO reports to the appropriate agency: 1. Air Force Regulation 200–2; 2. JANAP 146; 3. UFO Project Record Card." [7] Some of these restrictions apparently impose fines or courts-martial on Air Force personnel for disclosing UFO information. [8]

Several years ago I talked with a U.S. Air Force pilot who received a call from a ground radar station while he was flying his F–84 Sabre Jet over Vermont. The radar station had spotted a blip on the screen which it could not identify, and the pilot was asked to check it out—a fairly routine assignment. The pilot told me that as he closed in on the silvery metallic object, it suddenly accelerated away from him, and he could not catch it, despite the fact that he was flying the fastest jet in production at that time. He was convinced that the UFO was a spaceship from another world. Fortunately, I do not know his name, for I do not think that he was supposed to disclose this information. I have, of course, no way of knowing that the pilot was telling me the truth. But this contact was personally important for me because it tended to support what men such as Keyhoe and Edwards maintain; that is, that it is Air Force personnel who have the only overall picture of the UFO situation. Any UFO investigation by the University of Colorado without the full co-operation of the Air Force can hardly be complete.

Frank Edwards made the following statement in his book *Flying Saucers—Serious Business:*

> One night early in October of 1965, I addressed an audience of radar experts who had hired me, at their own expense, to come and tell them all that I could about the ubiquitous Unidentified Flying Objects. These were the men (Air Traffic Controllers) who see these things on their radar screens. These are the same men who are required by regulation to give out prefabricated answers or "explanations" to all who make inquiry about such things.
>
> Why were they paying me, a civilian newsman, to tell them about things they see more frequently than anyone else in the nation?
>
> The reason was simple: Although they were under the Federal Aviation Agency, that agency refused to answer their queries for information on the UFO's.[9]

Thus, even individual members of the Air Force network who have contact with UFOs do not have the total picture; only the few men at the top of Project Blue Book

can see the whole UFO landscape. Any university investigation which hopes to succeed will need to share this
view "from the top."

There are two reasons why it is for the "good of our
nation" to keep UFO information secret. (1) There is
the fear of public panic, and the possible economic crisis
on the stock market. (2) If UFOs exist, and are space
vehicles from another world, they seem to operate according to some antigravitational principle. Donald Keyhoe
devotes one chapter of his *Flying Saucer Conspiracy* to
the "Anti-G Field," and Edwards and others seem to agree
that some antigravitational (anti-G) force is at work in
UFOs. The nation which discovers the secret of antigravitational propulsion will have made a breakthrough
at least as important as the development of atomic energy,
and therefore anti-G information in connection with UFOs
would be "Top Secret." [10] I am not qualified to speak concerning the validity of the antigravitation hypothesis in
regard to UFOs, but given the suggestion that an anti-G
field is associated with modern UFOs, we shall discover
some fantastic consequences for Biblical studies, especially
when we examine the parting of the "Red Sea" during the
Exodus.

I cannot prove whether or not UFOs exist. The whole
issue must be settled by the very few men who are in a
position to collect and evaluate the data. There are at
present two schools of thought concerning UFOs: the one
which the Air Force maintains—either honestly or dis-
honestly—that UFOs do not exist, at least in the sense
that they are space craft from another world; and the
other position of Keyhoe, Edwards, and others that UFOs

or flying saucers do exist and that they are under the control of beings from another world.

A typical newspaper report of a UFO sighting is as follows:

> Two Erie [Pa.] newsmen said they saw and photographed early today a bright object in the sky near where a young couple reported the landing of a mysterious object.
>
> Dennis Buckel of radio station WJET said at about 2 a.m. he saw what looked like a bright star moving fast.
>
> Another WJET newsman, Jerry Trembley, said he saw the same object about two hours later and another cluster of flashing lights.
>
> On Sunday, Betty Jean Klem, 16, of Jamestown, N.Y., and Douglas Tibbets, 18, of Greenhurst, N.Y., said they saw a metallic, silvery object land near their car on a beach in Presque Isle State Park, a peninsula jutting into Lake Erie.
>
> Police said they found two triangular impressions in the sand, about 6 inches deep.
>
> The WJET newsmen came up with motion pictures of objects in the sky.[11]

This particular report does not mention the shape of the UFO, although many are of course described as saucer shaped. But the objects usually seem to give off light, travel at high speed, and are "silvery" in appearance. One can argue that the observers were not qualified, or that the motion pictures were faked, or that they in fact saw an artificial satellite—which does not, of course, account for the triangular impressions in the sand. Many UFO sightings never are printed. This one was printed because, although there may be doubt as to what was seen, several separate witnesses reported seeing a strange object; there

61

seems to be a good possibility that something strange was seen.

FLYING SAUCERS AND DEMYTHOLOGIZING

If flying saucers do exist, and if proof of their existence is eventually established, theologians attempting to develop a realistic Biblical interpretation will have one good historic example of how "demythologizers" have drawn premature conclusions. Anyone who accepts the Air Force position regarding UFOs assumes that flying saucers are a *mythological* or psychological construction of a group of "gullible" or mentally unbalanced people.

If we take as an example reporting which supports the Air Force position, a series of *Time* magazine articles exemplify what I have in mind. The well-known UFO sighting near Ann Arbor, Michigan, in March of 1966 was reported in the April 1 issue of *Time,* which included in its report a comment from a three-year-old girl who expected to "see a spaceman with 'green, yellow and orange-juice hair.'" The sighting was "a sure sign of primaveral delirium." The only sign of sanity was that "Through its Project Blue Book, the Air Force had looked into 10,147 other Unidentified Flying Objects since flying saucers entered American *mythology* [my italics] in 1947. . . . At week's end the Air Force attributed the Ann Arbor and Hillsdale apparitions to marsh gas (methane) created by organic decomposition and ignited by combustion." [12]

The following issue of *Time* reported what was called "The Gullibility Experiment." Some ingenious Students at Pasadena's California Institute of Technology sent aloft some brightly lighted balloons at night, and numerous

UFO reports resulted, thus proving how "gullible" every-one is.[13] I think it fair to point out that it is not every night that students launch lighted balloons into the sky. Further-more, people were actually seeing something when they made their reports. The students did not make their ex-periment until nearly two decades after "flying saucers" were first widely reported. One could very easily, on the basis of the students' experiment, draw the following con-clusion: when people see obviously strange UFOs in the sky, they will report them.

As an illustration of how an editor can support his per-sonal convictions, the Ann Arbor report was listed by *Time* as a "local" phenomenon under the heading "Na-tion," while the "Gullibility Experiment" was reported under "Science." I would not argue that everything re-ported as a UFO is in fact a flying saucer. Undoubtedly there is much mythology connected with UFOs, but just as in the gullibility experiment the reports did have some basis *in fact*, so I am very suspicious that the idea of flying saucers has some basis in fact.

As an illustration of the fact that the "marsh gas" theory is built on a swampy foundation, the Air Force scientist who put forward the theory was J. Allen Hynek, and he later wrote an article entitled "Are Flying Saucers Real?" for the December 17, 1966, issue of the *Saturday Evening Post*. In this article Hynek confesses that he had very little scientific fact to support his "swamp gas" conjecture, and he never intended it to be "the" answer to the Michi-gan sighting. After learning about swamp gas, Hynek says that he decided "it was a 'possible' explanation I would offer to the reporters." Hynek apparently did not even believe the explanation himself, and on the basis of the *Post* article, it is quite clear that Hynek believes the whole UFO problem to be far more complex than the simple "mythological" explanation such as *Time* magazine has assumed.[14]

Speaking of gullibility, I think one could as easily argue that *Time* is hardly showing intelligent skepticism in gleefully reporting the findings of an Air Force-sponsored scientist (the same Air Force which never heard of a U–2) who several days after the Ann Arbor sighting concluded that what was seen by dozens of witnesses—but not by the scientist—was swamp gas.

It does not seem to have occurred to anyone on the *Time* staff that a flying saucer might actually have been seen; there simply has to be another explanation—the flying-saucer answer is *a priori* out of the question. Anything—including swamp gas—is a more acceptable answer to those who must "demythologize" flying saucers. One irony is that the cover of the *Time* issue which reported the gullibility experiment raised the ominous question in red letters on black, "Is God Dead?" This issue devotes a considerable amount of space to the "God is dead" theology, which *Time* reports is led by "principally Thomas J. J. Altizer of Emory University" among others.[15] Demythologizing the Biblical material is one of the most important steps in the "God is dead" theology of Altizer. A scholar who has made pioneering studies concerning the mythological foundations of religion is Mircea Eliade, who has written among other works *The Sacred and the Profane*.[16] Thomas J. J. Altizer was a student of Eliade, and has written the study, *Mircea Eliade and the Dialectic of the Sacred*. Altizer relies heavily on the psychology of Carl G. Jung, as this work illustrates, and Eliade in works such as *Myths, Dreams and Mysteries: The Encounter Between Contemporary Faiths and Archaic Realities* also draws insights from the studies of Jung. I mention Jung because we have now come full circle. One of Jung's books is entitled *Flying Saucers: A Modern Myth of Things Seen in the Skies.*[17]

Again, I would not deny that UFOs, or at least UFO reports, exhibit many "mythological" characteristics. It does not add to the credibility of a well-reported article by Harold H. Deneault, Jr., entitled "Anatomy of a UFO Cover-Up," that the article appears on the cover of *Fate* magazine sandwiched between two articles under the titles, "Is Bhajan Singh Reborn in Munesh?" and "Thumping Poltergeist in California."[18] Undoubtedly many UFO reports are mythological in origin, but one thing which tends to separate UFOs from poltergeists is the frequency with which they are reported. To my knowledge, the U.S. Air Force has never considered carrying out a twenty-year investigation of poltergeists. Thus the flying-saucer debate is over the question: Do saucers exist, or are they myth? The modern theological debate is over several questions such as: Did Jesus rise from the dead, were "angels" present at the tomb, did Jesus ascend into space, or is this myth?

If sometime in the future we should finally have sufficient evidence to show beyond reasonable doubt that flying saucers do exist, I believe that this will automatically have important consequences for theology, whether or not modern UFOs have anything to do with the Bible. The demythologized "honest to God" theology of Robinson and the "death of God" theology of Altizer are rooted in three basic sciences: psychology, mythology, and philosophy (I use the term "science" in its broadest sense here). Starting with Bultmann, who assumed that the Biblical people held a "primitive" cosmology, theologians have then taken studies by men such as Eliade in religious myth and applied them to the Bible. The cause behind such mythology is interpreted in terms of psychological studies by scholars such as Jung, and theologians such as Bultmann, Robinson, or Altizer then draw from the existential philosophy of thinkers such as Martin Heidegger or Jean-Paul Sartre to reintepret the Biblical religion for modern man. There is a fantastic field of scholarship behind this theology which has made a valuable permanent impact on the twentieth century.

The basic question I have in mind, however, is as follows: Have the psychologically oriented existential demythologizers in theology tried to include too much in their world view? In the past we may have confused fact with myth. Are we now confusing myth with fact? By this I mean that this school of theology has built a triangular fortress with mythology, psychology, and existential philosophy serving as the three cornerposts. This theological fort seems to have contracted a disease similar to suburban sprawl, covering larger and ever larger areas within the triangle until now the point has been reached where these theologians claim that God may be dead. Have they now extended the boundaries of their demythologized theological fort too far? If they have, how can this be demonstrated? Suppose that Jung is wrong in his assumption that flying saucers are an example of a modern myth of things seen in the skies. This would mean that even such an eminent psychologist as Jung does not always know a myth when he sees one. If Jung is wrong about flying saucers,

then the "psychological" and "mythological" cornerposts
of demythologized Christianity may be shaken. The "existential" post depends on the other two posts for its
strength. If the other posts retreat, the existential post
will follow. The Bible suggests that Jesus "ascended" in
some sort of UFO. Theologians and psychologists can explain everything from the "Ascension of Christ" to "flying
saucers" in terms of "myth." But if flying saucers exist,
then perhaps we can again argue for a realistic interpretation of the Ascension of Christ (honestly).

Suppose that in a remote and primitive tribe of people
somewhere on earth a native ran excitedly into his village
and reported to his chief that he had just seen floating
down from the sky an "angel" suspended beneath a great
white sheet. The chief might call a council meeting, and
the tribal "psychologist" might suggest that the reporter
of the UFO had suffered a hallucination; the "demythologizer" would agree in part, but he would go on to say
that this "myth" of a man floating down from the sky
represents the reporter's psychological need to make contact with the transcendent and that he has given this need
an external mythological expression. The "existentialist,"
once he had heard the analysis of the psychologist and
the demythologizer, would go on to reassure the reporter
that while he did not actually see a man floating down
from the sky, nevertheless this myth could be given an
existential interpretation from which the whole tribe could
benefit, for in this way all could gain insight into their
"ground of being." If the "medicine man" in the tribe
(realistic or empiricist theologian) had not spoken by this
time, he would be well advised not to speak, for he is out-
numbered three to one. But the medicine man might gain

courage if a stranger carrying a parachute were then to wander into camp. If flying saucers do exist, and if we finally gain sufficient evidence of their existence to put the issue beyond doubt, then I dare say that the course of theology may be radically changed. If flying saucers do not exist, then much theology will probably continue its present course which leads down the road to the death of God. I am writing this book on the assumption that future evidence will point to the existence of flying saucers, but only time will put the question beyond reasonable doubt.

A good synthesis of the psychological, existential, and mythological studies of our time is found in Thomas J. J. Altizer's *Mircea Eliade and the Dialectic of the Sacred.* The "dialectic" about which Altizer speaks is between the sacred and the profane, which is roughly a dialectic between opposites, the mythological (sacred) and material (profane). To link flying saucers with the religious, of course, shatters the dialectic which Altizer wishes to establish, for it is quite likely that UFOs are material, not mythological. If flying saucers are material, there is for Altizer no way that they could be sacred. In his volume on Eliade we can see almost all the significant forces which have molded modern theology simultaneously at work. In his "Introduction" Altizer announces that:

> the moment has arrived to engage in a radical quest for a new mode of religious understanding. The first requirement of such a quest is a forthright confession of the death of God of Christendom, a full acknowledgment that the era of Christian civilization has come to an end, with the result that all cognitive meaning and all moral values that were once historically associated with the Christian God have collapsed. Furthermore, we must recognize that the death

of God is a historical event: God has died in *our* time, in *our* history, in *our* existence. Insofar as we live in our destiny, we can know neither a trace of God's presence nor an image of his reality.[19]

The Christian God is meaningless for most persons in the twentieth century, both intellectually and morally. But the question must be raised: Does the fault lie with God (being either dead or nonexistent), or does the fault lie with us, with the fact that our modern "scientific world view" has kept us from understanding the Biblical God realistically? Altizer has turned to Eliade as a source for a new understanding of the sacred because the Christian understanding is dead. Eliade has done his best work with Eastern religions, especially with Indian and Greek thought. The orientation of Eliade's thought is toward the soul, mind, or psyche. The soul is the seat of the sacred; the world is profane and, so far as the soul is caught up in worldliness, it is caught up in the profane. Modern science is grounded in "worldliness," and there is throughout Altizer's work a hostility toward science, which is extremely significant. Thus Altizer, like Eliade, "has long been attracted to Jung, while maintaining a bitter hostility toward Freud. Eliade objects to Freud's ideology, to his positivist understanding of 'pure sexuality,' for Freud refused to acknowledge the sacred dimension of psychic energy, of libido." [20]

Existentialists are generally hostile toward "positivism," and while I would not want to defend Freud or positivism at every point, I do think that the hallmark of positivism —sense experience—will eventually erode much of the foundation upon which the theological fort of Altizer and the death of God theologians has been constructed.

It is ironic that much of the stimulus behind the "death of God" theology has come from modern science—whether it be the demythologizing of the "three-decker universe" or our psychological interpretation of dreams and myths —and that theologians such as Altizer seem somewhat hostile toward the worldly methods of modern science. We may never again understand the Bible in the exact sense which our forefathers did; our understanding may have to mature, and psychological studies by men such as Eliade and Altizer may help this maturation. But if I understand Altizer correctly, he believes that the basic stimulus behind the Biblical religion was *internal*—within man's psyche; man was reaching out for God. I suggest that the basic stimulus behind the Biblical religion was *external*— in the particular embodiment of a group of beings from another world who deliberately brought about the Biblical religion; through these beings God was reaching for man. I agree that much of the Biblical material can be explained in psychological terms. But I think that the "honest to God" and "death of God" theologies have made one basic mistake: they have demythologized and psychologized *angels,* the messengers from another world, and all they imply.

To return to the "primitive camp" into which an airplane pilot has just parachuted, Bishop Robinson and Thomas Altizer are convinced that no stranger carrying a parachute will ever wander into our camp. They assume that a demythologized Christian faith must now be accepted as fact. To fly in the face of this fact amounts to intellectual dishonesty. In a newspaper report, Ian McLennan, "director of the proposed Strasenburgh Planetarium of the Rochester Museum of Arts and Sciences," in his review of Frank Edwards's *Flying Saucers—Serious Business*, admitted that "something has been happening in the sky—hundreds of thousands of people cannot make independent observations of the same optical phenomenon over thousands of square miles under a fantastic dose of mass hysteria." [21] But McLennan cannot feel certain about what is being seen. I believe that this is representative of the feeling of the scientific community at the present time —they admit that something is being seen, but scientists try to be careful not to mythologize the visible. Norton T. Novitt has suggested that a large body of flying ants might glow by attracting an electrical charge.[22] Together with stars, swamp gas, and clouds, there are any number of possible UFO explanations. But McLennan thinks it quite "probable" that there is life on other planets in the universe. Thus it is possible within the framework of modern science to suggest that beings from another world could have been part of the Biblical environment, although most scientists would undoubtedly consider it unlikely. But it is possible. Bishop Robinson finds amusement at the thought that the Bible seems to picture "a God 'out there' coming to earth like some visitor from outer space." [23] Precisely. A haunting thought, is it not? How would primitive people react if they made contact with visitors from another world? The Bible suggests that Jesus came from another world and that he returned to that world in a "cloud." It may be worth our time to look more closely at these Biblical "clouds."

CHAPTER III

THE OLD
TESTAMENT AND
FLYING SAUCERS

Some Observations on Exodus

The early Genesis material goes back several thousand years B.C., and Hebrew history which officially begins with Abraham may go as far back as 2000 B.C. There is no use pretending that Abraham (assuming that one admits he was a historical figure) held the same world view as a twentieth-century suburban American. There is no doubt that something like a "mythological" world view was shared by many ancient cults, and the Hebrew people mixed with this mythology, whether in Egypt or among the pagan tribes of Palestine. Our social sciences are built on the assumption that man is conditioned by his environment, and we can hardly expect that the Hebrews were unaffected by the cultures with which they were forced to mix. But one thing that is clear about the Hebrews is the fact that they did not mix very well with the rest of society, and many of the orthodox still prefer not to mix even up to the present day. The other fact is that one cannot make any strict rules about the religious environment which "conditioned" the Hebrew faith. The Bible suggests that the real environmental stimulus behind the Hebrew faith was a God who made himself known through agents from another world. Furthermore, the main evolution of the Biblical tradition seems to have been formed—according to the Biblical witness—in the wilderness between Egypt and Palestine, apart from any direct contact with a pagan society; but the scene in which Aaron makes the golden calf (Exodus 32:1–10) illustrates that the Hebrews did not easily escape from their past.

What happened in the wilderness? Was Moses a great religious thinker who in a powerful way got at least a band of Israelites free from Egypt, led them in the wilderness and, in the context of this situation, occasionally went up to high mountains to think out his religious program? Were the mountaintop experiences of Moses eventually "mythologized" to give those experiences the aura of deity? Or, as the Bible suggests, were the Hebrews in the wilderness under the stimulus and control of beings from another world who were deliberately seeking—for whatever motives—to plant a particular religious viewpoint within the minds of the Hebrews? Bishop Robinson argues (together with those scholars whose work he has synthesized) that just as the past century fought the battle over the scientific validity of the Creation material in Genesis, so now we shall have to fight to set the Exodus stories and the New Testament narratives free from their "mythological" world view. Robinson asks: "Is it necessary for the Biblical faith to be expressed in terms of this world-view, which in its way is as primitive philosophically as the Genesis stories are primitive scientifically?" [1]

Thus, the Biblical faith attributes itself to the intervention of beings from another world. Is this necessary? I would say that it is necessary only if it is true. Bishop Robinson assumes that such a view is out of the question. I say that it must be given serious attention. From a philosophical point of view, I doubt the ease with which Robinson moves from saying that the Genesis Creation stories are myth to implying that the Red Sea episode or the Ascension of Christ is mythological. From an empirical point of view, no one could have *witnessed* the Creation. Whatever else one says about the Creation story, it was not told by a man who had seen Creation. But the parting of the Red Sea, and the Ascension of Christ, are reported as if they were sense experiences—and we cannot rule out this possibility *a priori*, as we can with the Creation material. The Bible reports that Jesus was crucified, but I do not hear Bishop Robinson arguing that this is a mythological belief of the early Church. Everyone assumes that some of the eyewitness descriptions in the Scriptures have a right to be interpreted in a realistic way. The fact that many pagan religions were mythological does not automatically mean that the Christian faith is basically mythological. It is a live hypothesis to suppose that the beings from another world mentioned in the Bible were the *cause* behind the Biblical religion; although it may be easier to believe in the Crucifixion than the Ascension of

Christ, there seems to be no reason why both—in the light of the space age—could not have been witnessed events of the same order. There is an essential unity in the course of a person's day if he both witnesses a man knocked down by a car as he crosses a street, and sees a man board an airplane and fly off into space. Although the two events are not identical, there does not seem to be any necessary reason why the Crucifixion and Ascension reports should be separated.

The means by which the Old Testament patriarchs receive knowledge of God is not homogeneous. God sometimes seems to contact men through a vision in a dream during sleep as with Abimelech (Genesis 20:1–7), or a man may go into something like a trance or deep sleep as did Abraham (Genesis 15:12). These contacts are open to psychological interpretation, as psychologists such as Jung have shown. It is of course possible that reported *visual* contacts with beings from another world were in fact psychological projections—but this is not necessarily the case. When direct contact with beings from another world is made, the Bible often speaks as if direct contact had been made with God, as when three angels came to meet Abraham by his tent. "And the Lord appeared to him [Abraham] by the oaks of Mamre, as he sat at the door of his tent in the heat of the day. He lifted up his eyes and looked, and behold, three men stood in front of him" (Genesis 18:1,2). These three men came to Abraham with information that Sarah, despite her age, would conceive and bear a son. These men were so realistic that they ate a meal which Abraham prepared; Sarah laughed when she heard that she would conceive. On another occasion we find Jacob wrestling with a man all night—we discover that he is no ordinary man when the angel in desperation uses his "supernatural" power to touch Jacob's hip and put it out of joint (Genesis 32:24–25). It is interesting that these beings are described as men. They do not seem to have wings—they seem quite ordinary up to a point. Where do they come from and who are they?

When Abraham had made the covenant (contract) with God, he was ordered to prepare on an altar an offering of pieces of slaughtered animals, which God would then receive as a sign that God's signature had been placed on the contract. After the offering was prepared, and it was dark, "behold, a smoking fire pot and a flaming torch passed between these pieces" (Genesis 15:17), presumably consuming the offering. Biblical scholars have been able only to conjecture as to the meaning of this "smoking fire pot" and "flaming torch." Is it simply cultic symbolism, or was something strange happening here?

Jacob was sleeping on one occasion, and he dreamed "that there was a ladder set up on the earth, and the top of it reached to heaven; and behold, the angels of God were ascending and descending on it" (Genesis 28:12). Since the Bible describes this as a dream, we will exclude it from our list of passages which might be sense descriptions, but it is an interesting dream. Jacob seems to have met angels on many occasions when he was awake, and on one occasion he met so many that he said, "This is God's army" (Genesis 32:2).

Until the Exodus from Egypt, the Israelites do not really have a religion. They are simply living on a promise. One fundamental question about the Biblical religion is why Egypt should be willing to give up its slave labor—assuming that the Biblical witness is reliable at this point. And once the Israelites were out of Egypt, why did the Exodus-Leviticus-Numbers-Deuteronomy tradition evolve?

The Exodus begins when "the angel of the Lord" appears to Moses in the wilderness and calls to him "out of the midst of a bush" (Exodus 3:2). We shall return to this passage later, but it is worth noting that the "angel" speaks directly for God himself, much as the later prophets such as Isaiah speak for God. Moses was commissioned to get the Israelites out of Egypt and was apparently given unusual powers by which to do this; finally the first-born of Egypt were all killed on the famous "passover" night, and Pharaoh set Israel free. Scholars have not been able to agree how many Israelites marched from Egypt, but the Bible suggests a very large number along with cattle and possessions. The Exodus account goes on to relate that Pharaoh pondered the situation and decided that he had made a mistake in freeing his slaves. He pursued the Israelites with his army in an attempt to reclaim them.

At no point is the Exodus story ordinary, but at this juncture the scene becomes most extraordinary. The Bible narrates that "when Pharaoh let the people go . . . God led the people round by the way of the wilderness toward the Red Sea" (Exodus 13:17,18). What is meant by saying that God led the Israelites? Here is the answer. The "Lord went before them [the Israelites] by day in a pillar of cloud to lead them along the way, and by night in a pillar of fire to give them light, that they might travel by day and by night; the pillar of cloud by day and the pillar of fire by night did not depart from before the people" (Exodus 13:21,22). By means of an "Unidentified Flying Object," God led the Israelites from Egypt to the Red Sea.

How does this Biblical UFO compare with modern

UFOs? Modern UFOs sometimes exhibit a corona effect, which results in a white cloudlike halo appearance. Modern UFOs also usually glow in the dark, as the Biblical "pillar of fire by night" seems to have done. But the difficult question is the significance of the Hebrew term for *pillar*. There are in fact two Hebrew words which have been translated *pillar* in the RSV: *'ammūd* and *mazzēbāh*. In this passage the word *'ammūd* is used, which may mean a cylindrical column; thus the implication would seem to be that this UFO looked like a cylindrical column (height not specified), cloudlike during the day, but glowing in the dark. It is not clear whether the "pillar of cloud" stood vertically before the Hebrews or traveled horizontally in relation to the ground. Jacques Vallee, in his work *Anatomy of a Phenomenon: Unidentified Objects in Space; A Scientific Appraisal,* has found that in addition to the UFOs of the "flying-saucer" type, there is also clearly a *class* of UFOs (i.e., so many of this type have been seen and described that they form a separate class from the flying-saucer type) which "appear as huge cylindrical forms surrounded by cloud-like formations, often vertical." [2] If the Bible is describing a UFO which appears as a cloud-like cylindrical column during the day and as a glowing cylindrical column at night, then this UFO corresponds in description with a class of modern UFOs which have been seen with considerable frequency. Occasionally these cylindrical or "pillar" UFOs seem to act as a kind of "mother ship" for the flying-saucer type or class of UFO, which seem smaller in dimension than the pillars from which they come.

But this is by no means the only possible interpretation of the Hebrew understanding of the "pillar of cloud." G. A.

Barrois has pointed out that "the miraculous pillar plays, on a supernatural level, a function similar to that of Jacob's massebah as a testimony to God's presence." [3] On one occasion Jacob used a rock for a pillow; he had a dream of God during the night, so he set up the rock as a "pillar"—a witness or *mazzēbāh*—and this rock, since he used it as a pillow, might have had a flatter, more saucerlike shape than the cylindrical type of pillar (Genesis 28:18). When Jacob made a covenant with Laban, "they took stones, and made a heap" (Genesis 31:46) or pillar as a witness. This heap might have appeared conical, or like a turtle back, or perhaps like an upside-down saucer. Thus it is possible to argue that the "pillar of cloud" was a witness pillar in function, and that it may have physically resembled a flying saucer. It could be argued that the Biblical authors chose the word *'ammūd* rather than *mazzēbāh*, because the *mazzēbāh* became associated with the idols of the enemies of Israel and the Jews were under orders to smash these idols, "utterly overthrow them and break their pillars in pieces" (Exodus 23:24). Thus it is possible to argue that the "pillar of cloud" was a UFO which corresponds in description to *either* one of two classes of modern UFOs: the cloudlike cylindrical-column class (*'ammūd*), or the glowing flying-saucer class (*mazzēbāh*).

This Biblical UFO apparently leads the Israelites throughout their forty-year journey through the wilderness, according to the testimony of the book of Exodus, and the description of this UFO is by no means consistent. Sometimes the pillar of cloud is referred to as the "Lord" (Exodus 13:21; 14:24); other references seem to be "the angel of God" (Exodus 14:19), "the cloud" (Exodus 14:20), "the pillar of fire and of cloud" (Exodus 14:24), "the glory [brightness] of the Lord appeared in the cloud" (Exodus 16:10), "I am coming to you in a thick cloud" (Exodus 19:9, 16), "Mount Sinai was wrapped in smoke, because the Lord descended upon it in fire" (Exodus 19:18), "thick darkness" (Exodus 20:21), "an angel" (Exodus 23:20), "my angel" (Exodus 23:23; 32:34), "the cloud covered the mountain" (Exodus 24:15), "the glory of the Lord settled on Mount Sinai" (Exodus 24:16), "my presence will go with you" (Exodus 33:14), "the Lord descended in the cloud" (Exodus 34:5), and "So Moses finished the work. Then the cloud covered the tent of meeting" (Exodus 40:33–38). Thus it appears that during the whole of the Exodus the Israelites were accompanied by some sort of UFO, which receives its clearest description at the beginning of the Exodus, between Egypt and the Red Sea. Because of its various names, it is certainly difficult to come to a definite conclusion about the shape and size of the UFO, but on many occasions, as with its description as a "pillar of cloud and of fire," it seems to fit one of two classes of modern UFOs, either the cylindrical or the flying-saucer type. At this point it does not seem useful to decide in favor of one type over the other. Both are possible; the important question is, What did the Biblical UFO have to do with the Exodus?

The Bible suggests that this UFO, which seemed cloud-like during the day but which glowed in the dark, served as a beacon or guide which led the Israelites day and night from Egypt to the Red Sea. This UFO deliberately led the Israelites to the Red Sea, which seemed like a foolish thing to have done, because with the Egyptian army coming up from behind, the Hebrews were literally caught between Pharaoh and the deep blue sea. The Bible says

Pharaoh thought the Israelites were "entangled in the land; the wilderness has shut them in" (Exodus 14:3). Pharaoh and his army moved in for the kill, with the "pillar" having proved a poor guide, unless the being in charge of the UFO knew ahead of time what would happen at the Red Sea!

The Israelites were convinced that they were finished. They said to Moses, "Is it because there are no graves in Egypt that you have taken us away to die in the wilderness?" (Exodus 14:11) But as Pharaoh's army moved in, God's angel in the UFO took command of the situation. "Then the angel of God who went before the host of Israel moved and went behind them; and the pillar of cloud moved from before them and stood behind them, coming between the host of Egypt and the host of Israel. And there was the cloud and the darkness; and the night passed without one coming near the other all night" (Exodus 14:19, 20).

The text suggests that some sort of UFO, totally under its own control, led the Israelites out of Egypt to the Red Sea, and then as Pharaoh's army closed in, the UFO moved from the front to the rear of the army of Israel and kept the two military camps separated during the night. Is this history, myth, or a combination of both? The Bible does not say that Moses had some of his soldiers start a smudge-pot fire between the Israelites and the Egyptians. Is the Bible weaving a mythology out of a half-truth; did the Israelites somehow save themselves, or was there really some sort of UFO under intelligent control which deliberately sought to save Israel from Egypt?

Phase one of the operation involves leading Israel to the sea; phase two requires the UFO to keep the camps separate until darkness falls. Now begins phase three. "Then Moses stretched out his hand over the sea; and the Lord drove the sea back by a strong east wind all night, and made the sea dry land, and the waters were divided" (Exodus 14:21). (When we argue that the Israelites were on the shore of the "Red Sea," we are simply using the Biblical designation from the Revised Standard Version. No one knows for certain which body of water was involved in the crossing, but the Hebrew seems to suggest a swampy "Sea of Reeds.") The best scholarship of our day agrees that the Israelites were moving from west to east. Martin Noth, in his *Exodus: A Commentary*, says that Israel may have camped on "the western shore of the Sirbonian Sea." [4] Since Israel was moving from Egypt to Palestine, from west to east, logic suggests that the Hebrews were on the *western* shore of some body of water, and an east wind would be blowing in the *faces* of the chosen people. *The Interpreter's Bible* has argued that "Since the wind is from the east we must assume that the crossing took place somewhere near the *eastern* shore of the sea or lake";[5] the editors of *The Interpreter's Bible* seem to have assumed—quite rightly—that any wind strong enough to cause the parting of the sea would prohibit the Israelites from crossing the sea if the wind were blowing in their faces. Thus, without any further argument, they have concluded that Israel was on the eastern shore heading back toward Egypt! But Martin Noth and others, and the logic of the Exodus, suggest that Israel was on the western shore with the wind blowing in the faces of her people.

There is almost no evidence that the Israelites were able to take advantage of an "accident" of nature. Noth has argued that there is no natural parallel to the Red Sea incident.[6] The other alternatives are to assume (1) that the whole sequence concerning the Red Sea is a fabrication; (2) that God somehow directly intervened in the situation in some unexplained way; or (3) that beings from another world were present in some sort of UFO and that they deliberately caused the sequence of events which the Bible narrates.

The Bible argues that the wind caused the sea to part. How did the persons present know that the wind caused the sea to part? They might have seen the sea part, and they might have felt the wind blowing, and concluded that the wind was the *cause* of the observed *effect*—the parting of the sea. But as every scientist knows, relating cause and effect can be a tricky business. It is no easy step to conclude that because a certain type of mosquito is present in a situation, it transmits malaria. The fact that a particular mosquito and malaria are present in the same situation may be mere coincidence. Thus we may very well trust the Biblical statement that the sea parted; we may also trust that there was an east wind blowing; but we are not thereby compelled to conclude that the wind caused the sea to part. Perhaps something *intangible* caused it to part.

There are several reasons why it is difficult to attribute the cause of the parting to the wind. Later in the sequence the sea falls back over the Egyptians and drowns them; they could hardly drown in only a couple of feet of water. Even if the sea were only ten feet deep at its deepest point, since water weighs about 62.4 pounds per cubic foot, at a depth of ten feet the water would be applying a pressure of 624 pounds per square foot on the bottom of the sea. It would seemingly take this amount of wind pressure per square foot to force the water back and maintain the opening. Since the Israelites were crossing, according to most scholars, from west to east, they would have to go against this powerful wind, with wives, children, and cattle. The Bible does not even mention any wind at all during the crossing. If the Israelites crossed in the face of a wind generating 624 pounds pressure per square foot, would this not be worth mentioning? Since man has about the same body density as water, it would appear that the people, like the water, would be thrown back by the wind. If the wind ceased to blow, why would the water not come back upon Israel?

The Bible goes on to describe the crossing of the sea "on dry ground" (Exodus 14:22). The Israelites knew that the water had been pushed back, but they seemed surprised— perhaps shocked—that the ground was dry. The Hebrew suggests that this was a "Sea of Reeds"; the area where the Israelites crossed may have been swampy, at least near each shore line. The Israelites undoubtedly expected that as soon as they stepped into the shore area, they would sink up to their ankles in mud. But they crossed on dry ground! Every farmer knows that a wind may dry off the surface of a newly plowed field, but it is a very slow process for the water two to six inches under the surface to evaporate. The Israelites expected to be wading in mud, when in fact the ground was dry and by implication hard. The Israelites were driving cattle, yet there is no mention that even their sharp hoofs cut through the surface soil of the sea bed. I do not believe that even a very strong east wind, blowing for part of an evening—without even the benefit of the heat of the sun—could dry out the underlying layer of mud.

The Bible also narrates that when the Israelites went into the sea, the waters were "a wall to them on their right hand and on their left" (Exodus 14:22). In poetic celebration the idea is emphasized: "the floods stood up in a heap" (Exodus 15:8). Some scholars are convinced that this idea is an "embellishment." If a wind were the cause of the parting of the sea, we could hardly expect a wall effect. The force of wind disperses, much as the impact of a pebble in a pond disperses in ever widening rings. If wind were to force the sea back, the result might be a very moderate concave effect, but certainly we would not expect a "wall" on each side. A wall suggests not only vertical sides but also smoothness, and the wind would create neither vertical walls nor a smooth surface.

When the army of Egypt pursued the Hebrews down into the trough of the sea created by the walls on each side, Moses was told to raise his hand over the sea, and the walls of the sea broke and came back upon the Egyptians (Exodus 14:26–29). If Moses is merely taking advantage of an "accident" of nature, it is certainly a fantastic accident that the winds would start blowing when he raised his rod and stop blowing at a later point when he raised his hand. But even more important, the Bible does not say that when Moses raised his hand the wind stopped blowing. There is no mention of any wind at all. Moses raised his hand and the water returned. There is no wind mentioned. The Israelites may have suspected that the Lord was using something besides wind to keep the walls of the sea in check.

In summary, a wind strong enough to force the sea back would make conditions impossible for crossing; the ground was apparently dry and hard for the crossing, which an evening's wind could hardly do; the water seems to have been held in a position resembling a wall—vertical and smooth—which wind could hardly do; and when Moses raised his hand for the water to return, no mention is made of the wind. It would seem that we are faced with a choice: if we want to believe that the *wind* caused the parting of the sea, then we cannot believe that vertical walls were formed, that the sea bed became hard and dry, or that it was likely that the starting and stopping of the wind would be instantaneous, as it seems to have been. The other alternative is to suppose that something other than the wind caused the parting of the sea so as to produce symptoms such as vertical walls of water.

There is no way that we can be true to the Biblical text and suppose that the Israelites took advantage of an "accident" of nature. If we want to explain everything as simply an act of God, then there is no need to discuss the text— presumably God can do anything. But there is a *tertium quid* worth exploring. The Biblical text makes it quite clear that some sort of UFO was in the vicinity of the Red Sea at the time it parted; if beings from another world were in the situation with the specific intention of saving the Israelites, let us see how the events described in Scripture can be reconciled with our knowledge of modern UFOs.

If a modern UFO were anxious to cause something like the parting of the Red Sea, it would probably use an anti-gravitational beam (anti-G beam), or something like an anti-G beam, to move the water back. Both Keyhoe and Edwards are convinced that our modern UFOs operate according to some antigravitational principle, although Vallee is not so certain. The positive gravitational power

87

of the moon orbiting the earth causes the tides in our oceans to rise; if the moon were to be endowed with an anti-G force, it would push the water in the oceans away from it rather than attracting water toward it. If a UFO were to hover over the body of water which the Israelites were to cross, and if it were to apply a sufficiently strong anti-G beam to the area which the Israelites desired to cross, the water would quite probably be forced back. Radio blackouts have been reported when UFOs have been near car radios, which indicates some kind of electromagnetic (EM) interference. UFOs are nearly silent when they move, another indication that their propulsion system could be "antigravitational" or "electromagnetic" in form, although modern science has not yet discovered how such a system would operate.

Until further evidence is available, let us suppose that UFOs operate by means of some sort of anti-G or EM beam, keeping in mind the speculative nature of this assumption. Light and gravity are both electromagnetic in nature, and it is interesting to compare some of the properties of light with gravity. Light can be focused in a "beam" by using a concave reflector, as is done with a flashlight or with automobile headlights. One should notice that these "reflectors" are almost "saucerlike" in shape. Radio telescopes, used to collect electromagnetic energy from distant stars, are sometimes referred to as "dishes" because of their "saucerlike" shape. Radar beams are sometimes focused by saucerlike reflectors. Probably all forms of electromagnetic energy can be focused into a beam by saucerlike reflectors. Flying saucers may be circular and saucerlike in shape in order to *focus* their electromagnetic

propulsion beam in much the same way we focus a flashlight beam.

According to an Associated Press newspaper report,
policemen and citizens in Wanaque, New Jersey, saw a
UFO which was "saucer-shaped, about the size of an
automobile and glowing with a white brilliance." One of
the policemen (Sergeant Thompson) "said he got out of
the car and continued to watch the object for almost five
minutes 'until the glowing light blinded me.'" The article
continued, "Thompson said the object maneuvered, stir-
ring up brush and water in the reservoir. 'It was about 150
feet up,' he said." [7] Frank Edwards has remarked about
the fact that UFOs have often been seen to cause a disturbance *in water directly under the flying saucer*.[8] How could
a UFO 150 feet in the air cause a disturbance in the water
beneath? An antigravitational or electromagnetic beam
seems capable of providing an acceptable answer.

Returning to the Biblical material, it seems necessary in
the light of our present knowledge of UFOs to find some
way to move the "pillar of cloud" from the position it took
between the armies of Israel and Egypt to a position directly over the sea. The Exodus narrative does not tell us
when the UFO moved over the sea. The Bible says that
after the cloud moved between the two armies, "there was
the cloud and the darkness" (Exodus 14:20). Martin Noth
in his commentary has observed the reference to the "darkness" and has suggested that there is the possibility that
the "pillar of cloud and fire" did not glow in the dark on
this particular night as it usually did.[9] As a general rule the
UFO seems to have given off enough light so that Israel
could march at night (Exodus 13:21), but this light might

also have enabled the Egyptians to overcome Israel at night. If on this one occasion the UFO did not glow at night, then the Israelites would not have seen the pillar of cloud move during the night to a position over the sea. Once it became dark, the Egyptians would be forced to set up camp; they would be willing to wait until morning for the battle, as the Israelites could hardly go anywhere with their backs to the sea. The next time the UFO was seen by Israel, it was in fact hovering over the sea, directly over the "channel" which had been formed for the crossing. The UFO became visible over the channel during the morning watch, at which time the sun might be giving enough light on the horizon so that the UFO could be seen even if it were not glowing (Exodus 14:24). The sea did not begin to part until it was dark (Exodus 14:21), and when it finally became light enough to see, the UFO was found hovering directly over the channel (Exodus 14:24). Thus on the basis of the Biblical text it is quite permissible to argue that the UFO hovered over the sea in order to cause it to part, and directly over the sea the anti-G or EM beam would be most effective.

It might be argued that the Bible does not say that the UFO caused the sea to part; the Lord, according to Exodus, caused the sea to part. But Martin Noth argues that at least in the "J" tradition the cause of the parting of the sea is the pillar of cloud.[10] We read that "the Lord in the pillar of fire and of cloud looked down upon the host of the Egyptians" (Exodus 14:24); if the Lord was "in" the pillar of cloud, and if the Lord caused the sea to part, then it would follow that the "efficient" cause (to use Aristotle's distinction) of the parting of the sea was somehow located in the UFO.

It might also be argued that modern UFOs, although they may disturb water directly under them, have never caused anything like the parting of the sea. This is of course true, but modern UFOs presumably use only enough anti-G or EM power to permit their mobility; they may on most occasions displace only the equivalent of their own weight in water through the beam. If a much more powerful anti-G or EM beam were to be focused on a body of water, I believe that there would be more than the relatively slight effects observed in modern times. One may then be compelled to ask: If modern UFOs are propelled by an anti-G beam, and if such a beam would be necessary to cause the Red Sea to part, what would stabilize the UFO over the sea while this powerful beam was applied? To pose the problem in another way, suppose that the anti-G or EM propulsion system of UFOs is compared with our rocket principles which operate according to Newton's third law of motion (i.e., for every action there is an equal and opposite reaction). A rocket or jet stream is focused in one direction, and the space vehicle is "pushed" by the rocket or jet in the opposite direction. Thus when an anti-G beam is focused toward the earth, the UFO is pushed like a rocket away from the earth. A very powerful rocket may completely leave the earth's gravitational field and travel into outer space. If a UFO were to apply a very powerful beam over the Red Sea, why would the UFO not be propelled like a rocket into outer space? The answer must be speculative, of course, but it should be noted that some modern UFOs have been described as "double-convex";[11] that is, they are saucer shaped on the top and on the bottom. If a rocket were equipped with a propulsion jet on the top and on the bottom, aimed in opposite directions, and if both were ignited at once, the rocket ship would not move—the two power jets would cancel each other out. When two automobiles traveling at the same speed meet in a head-on collision, both may come to an immediate stop. If a "double-convex" flying saucer were to focus equally powerful anti-G beams in opposite directions, the UFO would not move. This is speculation, but at present there does not seem to be any reason to say that UFOs do not have the technical capabilities of causing the sea to part through an anti-G or EM beam. Furthermore, there is nothing in the Biblical account which prohibits us from saying that the UFO *caused* the parting of the sea, or that it hovered above the sea at night while the channel was formed.

The Bible suggests that the ground was dry and by implication hard—free from mud. An antigravitational force would cause everything under it in effect to become heavier—two, three, or four times heavier. Not only would the water under the UFO be forced back, but the anti-G beam would be applying pressure to the remaining muddy sea bed. The effect would be like pushing a heavy lawn roller over a sponge. The dense mud would in effect become more dense, forcing the water in the mud to the surface and then forcing that water back with the dividing "walls." Another fact to be considered is that many people have experienced an intense heating effect when they have come directly under a UFO. This might be another side effect of the anti-G beam, because an electromagnetic beam might cause increased molecular activity in the body upon which it was focused, or the EM beam might be of such a frequency that heat is a natural form of energy release. If this effect were applied to the bed of the Red

Sea, the mud might very well be "baked" in much the same way pottery is baked; and this would also contribute to the fact that Israel seems to have been pleasantly surprised to cross on a dry, apparently hard surface, rather than having to wade up to their ankles in mud in the "Sea of Reeds." The "rolling" effect together with a "baking" effect could together account for the "dry ground."

Light is a form of electromagnetic energy, and it can be focused in a "beam" because light travels basically in a straight line. The Bible relates that the water was pushed back and formed a wall on each side of the Hebrews. If the UFO could control an anti-G or EM beam in much the same way we control a flashlight beam, we might expect that when the anti-G beam was applied to the Red Sea the water would be pushed back only as far as the area over which the beam was applied. Furthermore, since the electromagnetic anti-G beam would presumably travel, like light, in a straight line, the effect would be the forming of a wall of water on each side of the beam. This wall would not only be vertical, but would probably appear to have quite a smooth surface, almost as if a sheet of glass were placed against each wall of the sea to hold it back.

An anti-G beam would travel at about the speed of light, 186,000 miles per second, so that when Moses raised his hand as the signal for the anti-G beam to be turned off, the walls of water would begin to fall back on the Egyptians immediately. The anti-G beam allows for instantaneous response; it is much more efficient than a strong east wind.

The Bible does say that a strong east wind was blowing, at about the time the water was forced to divide and form the walls. What can we say about this? If the pillar of cloud and fire—the UFO—were hovering over the sea and applied an anti-G beam to the sea, everything under the UFO would become in effect heavier. Not only would the water be pushed back, and the mud be "rolled" dry, but the air directly under the beam would also become heavier, and would be forced down toward the sea bed directly under the UFO beam. The walls of water on each side would form a trough or channel, and when the air hit the sea bed, it would then shoot out each empty end of the channel formed by the two walls of water. If the Israelites were standing on the west bank ready to cross to the eastern shore, the wind would be hitting them right in the face as it came out of the channel—and they would report that a strong east wind was blowing. If they had been standing on the eastern bank, however, they would also have had a strong wind blowing toward them—but apparently from the west. (This wind would assist in drying off the surface of the sea bed.) As the air under the UFO was forced down, lighter air from above the UFO would be drawn down into the "semivacuum" created as the air under the UFO was pushed down. Thus a continuous stream of air current would result. Frank Edwards reports that one UFO as it was seen to ascend into the air from fairly near the ground caused dust to be kicked up from the ground.[12] If UFOs operate according to some anti-G principle, this may be an example of how the anti-G beam forces air currents down, thus causing the "dust" to fly.

There is one difficulty which must be considered, and for which there is only a theoretical answer. While it is true that a wind strong enough to part the Red Sea would be too strong to allow the Israelites with their families and possessions to cross, the anti-G beam presents similar problems. Everything under the anti-G beam would in effect become heavier. This would probably be true also for the Israelites as they moved under the beam; each man, woman, child, animal, and possession would seem to weigh several times its normal weight. If the Israelites noticed such an effect while crossing the sea, we would certainly expect them to report it; in fact, it might be impossible to cross under these conditions. We are therefore forced to assume that after the water was forced back and the sea bed became dry, part of the anti-G beam was shielded off so that the center area of the channel would be free of the anti-G effects. Sometimes the moon comes between the earth and sun in such a way as to cause an eclipse—the electromagnetic light radiation of the sun is shielded off by the moon. If beings from another world were operating a UFO in the Red Sea situation, it is certainly not only possible, but probable, that their technology permitted them to shield off part of the anti-G beam or anti-G jets while allowing two powerful walls of the anti-G beam to remain, one in front of each wall of water in the sea bed. While an anti-G beam may have been applied uniformly to the Red Sea to move the water back and to roll out and bake the mud, once the water was back in the desired position some of the beam could be phased out in the center of the desired crossing area so as to permit the Israelites to cross in total freedom.

Such an explanation might appear to be extremely hypothetical except for the sequence which the Bible relates after the Israelites have crossed safely to the eastern shore. As the morning light began to allow the Egyptians to see what was happening, they followed the Israelites with their chariots right into the channel of the sea. The Israelites were presumably high and dry on the other side, having completed the crossing, and they looked down into the channel and observed with concern the Egyptians in hot pursuit. Were the Hebrews nearly to have made this astounding escape only to be caught from behind as the Egyptians used the escape channel? No, for Moses would raise his hand as a signal for the walls to fall in on the Egyptians, but before the walls of water collapsed, something strange seemed to be happening to the Egyptians down in the channel. We read, "And in the morning watch the Lord in the pillar of fire and of cloud looked down upon the host of the Egyptians, and discomfited the host of the Egyptians, clogging their chariot wheels so that they drove heavily" (Exodus 14:24, 25). The King James Version is closer to the Hebrew than the RSV, however. It reads, "And it came to pass, that in the morning watch the Lord looked unto the host of the Egyptians through the pillar of fire and of the cloud, and troubled the host of the Egyptians. And took off their chariot wheels, that they drave them heavily" (Exodus 14:24, 25).

The Bible does not tell us when the UFO moved into a position directly over the sea bed. The last time we heard about the UFO it had settled down between the armies of Israel and Egypt. The Egyptians apparently set up camp and waited until morning to make the next move. Then the UFO moved over the sea under the cover of darkness, causing the sea to part. The Israelites did not see the UFO hovering over the channel until the first light of day, and by that time the Hebrews had completed their crossing and were looking down at the Egyptians in the trough of the sea.

The Egyptians were having some kind of difficulty, and the text suggests that the "pillar of cloud" was the cause of the crisis. The Egyptians were perhaps pointing up toward the UFO over their head, thus suggesting to the Israelites that whatever the distress, its cause was above them.

The Lord (or the angel of God) in the UFO looked down upon the Egyptians in the channel of the sea bed and "discomfited" or "troubled" the Egyptians. The Hebrew suggests that the Lord "looked" down upon the Egyptians with such a powerful force that he "crushed" them—to speak as the Bible sometimes does about a heavy heart suggests a "troubled" heart. The Egyptians seem to have been "crushed" or "troubled" or made "heavy" by the "looking down" of the Lord in the UFO above them. Apparently the UFO had somehow caused the Egyptians suddenly to become very heavy—the anti-G beam was once again applied to the whole area of the sea bed. The shield which had freed part of the sea bed from the anti-G beam so that the Israelites could cross was suddenly removed. This shield was not removed until many of the Egyptians had driven their chariots a considerable distance into the channel; otherwise they would in all likelihood not have been able to enter the trough at all. Everything seemed to be going well as the Egyptians pursued with their chariots down into the center of the channel, when suddenly the Lord "looked down" on the Egyptians and knocked them flat. They were crushed by an invisible weight.

The King James Version follows the Hebrew in telling us that the Lord in the UFO caused the wheels of the Egyptian chariots to come off. The RSV translators could not make sense of the Hebrew, so they turned to a Syrian word which suggested that the wheels of the chariots became "clogged." Probably the RSV translators assumed that the chariot wheels became stuck in the mud; but as was made very clear during the crossing of the Israelites, there was no mud to be found—they crossed on hard, dry ground. Where did the mud suddenly come from? Not only has the RSV been untrue to the Hebrew in suggesting that the chariot wheels were clogged rather than removed, but the idea of "mud" has been introduced, which the previous narrative strictly excludes. If the anti-G beam were once again applied to the whole sea bed, the chariots would suddenly weigh two to four times as much as normal, or more; the pressure on the axles of the chariots might well cause the axles to bend or break, thus removing the wheels. Furthermore, the narrative specifically draws attention to the UFO above as the cause of the difficulty, not to the mud below. The Lord "looked down" upon the chariots with a great force and broke off their chariot wheels.

Not only were the wheels removed, but the chariots appeared to drive "heavily." The Israelites on the shore saw the Egyptians suddenly knocked down or crushed by extra weight, and the chariot wheels were broken off. They also undoubtedly saw the horses either knocked to the ground by the extra weight, or at least straining greatly, so that the chariots appeared to drive "heavily"; everything, in fact, had suddenly become much heavier. In the face of these difficulties the Egyptians wisely concluded, "Let us flee from before Israel; for the Lord fights for them against the Egyptians" (Exodus 14:25). But this decision came too late for the Egyptians down in the channel; as soon as the anti-G beam was lifted, the waters came back upon the Egyptians. "The waters returned and covered the chariots and the horsemen and all the host of Pharaoh that had followed them into the sea; not so much as one of them remained. But the people of Israel walked on dry ground through the sea, the waters being a wall to them on their right hand and on the left" (Exodus 14:28, 29). If part of the anti-G beam had not been shielded off in order to allow the Hebrews to cross, they too would have been crushed by the same powerful "look" from the UFO which "discomfited" the Egyptians.

At this point it is worthwhile to examine and compare the value of the above interpretation of the Red Sea incident with other interpretations. There have been at least two attempts to link the pillar of cloud and of fire with some natural phenomenon. Martin Noth has suggested that when the Israelites came to Mount Sinai they met a volcano, and this volcano made such an impression on the Hebrews that they introduced the idea into the narrative of the whole Exodus story.[13] Of course a volcano cannot move around the way the Biblical UFO apparently does. In another interpretation, A. H. McNeile has suggested that ancient peoples sometimes marched "carrying braziers containing burning wood at the head of an army";[14] thus a burning smudge pot carried in front sent up a pillar of cloud to lead the army in a march. While this type of UFO is more mobile than a volcano, it is obviously a man-controlled entity, whereas the Hebrew narrative leaves no doubt that they were not controlling the "angel of God"; rather, the UFO was controlling them. They followed it. Of its own initiative it moved from in front of Israel to the rear to separate the Egyptian army from Israel. The UFO apparently caused the parting of the sea, and crushed the Egyptians under it in the channel. If scientists should eventually establish that UFOs exist and that they operate by means of some kind of anti-G or EM beam, then my interpretation would seem to have several advantages over either the "volcano" or the "smudge-pot" interpretation of the pillar of cloud and of fire. If we take as our starting assumption the basic Biblical testimony— that the Israelites were under the guidance of an external force—then we can assume that the being in charge of the pillar of cloud *knew ahead of time* that the army of Israel would be saved from Egypt by the parting of the sea, and all this implies. We are in a much better position to make sense of the narrative by assuming that whatever extraordinary things are involved in the Red Sea experience, the *direct* cause of these things lies in the UFO which seems to be in charge of the situation.

As in all Biblical narratives, we may ask the question: Did the Biblical story arise as a "mythological" fabrication of a fairly ordinary or even extraordinary human experience—was an unusual experience given a "mythological" religious perspective? Or was there really some external agent in the situation—in the UFO—which deliberately caused the unusual sequence of events which Exodus relates? If we do not believe that beings from another world in a UFO were in the situation, how did Israel escape from Egypt? Egypt was not anxious to give up its slave labor. We may even wonder about the various plagues which originally struck Egypt and brought Israel's freedom.

The only point at which we have not been true to the Biblical narrative is in saying that the *direct* cause of the parting of the sea was not the strong east wind. But there was apparently an east wind blowing out of the channel. Our interpretation is in fact true to all the "sense-data" which the Biblical narrative provides. Our only exception to the narrative is in point of theory—the Biblical connection between cause and effect, between the parting of the sea and the east wind. The "east wind" may well have distracted us from looking to the true source of the parting—to the UFO which hovered over the sea—to the angel of God in the pillar of cloud and of fire.

The Pillar of Cloud After the Red Sea

We cannot help being interested in the activity of this UFO—this pillar of cloud and of fire—after the sequence of events at the Red Sea. There was no doubt in the minds of the authors of the Biblical material that the UFO was intimately connected with the whole Red Sea narrative, which explains why the UFO is given such a prominent role at this juncture. Furthermore, the Bible maintains that this UFO was present during the whole of the Exodus, including the forty years in the wilderness. While the role of the UFO is never more dramatic than at the sea, there are several occasions on which the UFO plays a major role, which must now be examined.

The Israelites had not traveled far beyond the Red Sea when they discovered that they were in the middle of the wilderness without any source of food, and they began to think that they had been better off as slaves sitting by the "fleshpots" of Egypt (Exodus 16:3). But now the sea which had set Israel free from slavery stood in the way of a return to Egypt—and the fleshpots. But the UFO was still in charge, and the Lord said to Moses, "Behold, I will rain bread from heaven for you" (Exodus 16:4). Moses instructed Aaron to explain to the Israelites that the Lord would provide bread. "And as Aaron spoke to the whole congregation of the people of Israel, they looked toward the wilderness, and behold, the glory of the Lord appeared in the cloud" (Exodus 16:10). For the Biblical frame of mind, the bread which covered the earth like dew in the morning was somehow connected with, or caused by, the UFO which led Israel safely across the Red Sea. Clear also is the fact that the promise of bread from heaven would be fulfilled only if Israel followed the glory of the Lord— the bright cloud—into the wilderness. If you wanted bread, you had to follow the UFO. This "stimulus" and "response" conditioning is certainly in the best psychological tradition. In the book of Numbers we see quite clearly that the Israelites followed the cloud; "whenever the cloud was taken up from over the tent, after that the people of Israel set out; and in the place where the cloud settled down, there the people of Israel encamped" (Numbers 9:17).

Donald Keyhoe, in his work *The Flying Saucer Conspiracy*, devotes a chapter to what he calls "Angel Hair," which seems to be a fine flakelike substance which has been observed dropping from UFOs.[15] This "Angel Hair" sometimes, although not always, disintegrates when a person touches it, and it very often evaporates in the heat of the sun. Whether or not anyone has tried to eat this substance, I do not know! But the description of the "bread from heaven" is strikingly parallel. "And when the dew had gone up, there was on the face of the wilderness a fine, flake-like thing, fine as hoarfrost on the ground. When the people of Israel saw it, they said to one another, 'What is it?' [*manna*] For they did not know what it was" (Exodus 16:14, 15); "it was like coriander seed, white, and the taste of it was like wafers made with honey" (Exodus

16:31). And in the morning the Israelites gathered enough for their daily use, except on the sixth morning, when they gathered enough for two days; the Israelites did not gather every piece of "manna," or "what is it?" in sight, and "when the sun grew hot, it melted" (Exodus 16:21). If this is mythology, it is certainly interesting myth—the Israelites seem to have invented an imaginative bread from heaven so esoteric that they were hard pressed even to name it, so they called it "manna—what is it?"

This is further evidence that there really were beings from another world in the situation, and that the beings in the UFO were responsible for the distribution of some type of food which the Israelites were hard pressed to describe. It may be that the beings in the UFO "seeded" the air with a fine food dust which dropped to the ground, absorbing the dew; when morning sunshine provided light, perhaps the food dust worked like yeast and grew into the small "flake-like thing" which the Israelites ate. For our future space travel it will be useful to develop foods which, when combined with water, yield a substantial bulk. Moses on occasion provided water for the Israelites by striking a rock with his rod (Exodus 17:1–7), so it is not surprising that Moses was a powerful commander. It was after these various physical needs were met—freedom from Egyptian enslavement, freedom from hunger and thirst—that the beings in the UFO, the angels of God, proceeded to give the Hebrews a Law, a religion.

Thus the Sinai tradition, with its Ten Commandments, begins by saying, *because* "I am the Lord your God, who brought you out of the land of Egypt, out of the house of bondage," "You shall have no other gods before me" (Exodus 20:2, 3). Before the commandments were given,

Moses was told to gather the Israelites around the foot of Mount Sinai, because "the Lord will come down upon Mount Sinai in the sight of all the people" (Exodus 19:11). The Sinai tradition is very lengthy and is not easy to unravel, and we shall not attempt to clarify the textual problems. Moses apparently went up and down the mountain several times. He went to the top to talk with God—or with the angel of God (Exodus 23:20–23)—came down to talk to the people at the foot of the mountain, then returned to the top. Moses remained at the top of the mountain to talk with the angel of God for long intervals of time—the Bible suggests forty days and nights (Exodus 24:18), which is the Bible's way of saying a long time. In fact, Moses spent so much time on the mountain that the people became restless and started dancing and singing, making molten calves, and generally having a rollicking time; the people "rose up to play" (Exodus 32:6).

On at least one occasion a special demonstration of the power of God was displayed on Mount Sinai. The people were gathered around the foot, and then God descended on the mountain. "On the morning of the third day there were thunders and lightnings, and a thick cloud upon the mountain, and a very loud trumpet blast, so that all the people who were in the camp trembled. Then Moses brought the people out of the camp to meet God; and they took their stand at the foot of the mountain. And Mount Sinai was wrapped in smoke, because the Lord descended upon it in fire; and the smoke of it went up like the smoke of a kiln, and the whole mountain quaked greatly" (Exodus 19:16–18). This description has led scholars to suppose that the Hebrew people were witnessing volcanic activity, and the suggestion has been carried further that because of this volcanic experience the Jews developed their understanding of God on the basis of this experience.

But volcanic activity is not the only explanation which might fit this description. On November 2, 1957, just before midnight (according to Jacques Vallee), two men traveling on Highway 116 in Texas saw a "bluish-green torpedo-shaped machine 150 to 200 feet long which remained close to the ground for two or three minutes, then ascended, its color changing to red." The presence of the UFO had caused the motor of the truck to stop, and the headlights were cut off. The men gave this account:

> We first saw a flash of light in the field to our right, and we didn't think much about it—then it rose up out of the field and started toward us, picking up speed. When it got nearer, the lights of my truck went out and the motor died. I jumped out and hit the deck as the thing passed directly over the truck with a great sound and a rush of wind. It sounded like thunder, and my truck rocked from the blast. I felt a lot of heat. Then I got up and watched it go out of sight toward Levelland.[16]

The report of the "rush of wind" might be due to the movement of the ship, or to the downward thrust of the propulsion beam, as reported during the Red Sea episode. It is not impossible that a UFO of the type seen in Texas—torpedo-shaped, or like a pillar or cylinder—could have caused the flashing light, and the thunderings, and if the truck rocked from the blast of the UFO, perhaps the whole mountain would quake if a tremendous anti-G force were applied. The whole purpose of the Mount Sinai scene was to demonstrate to the Israelites the power of God, for at least three reasons: The people of Israel were about to receive a religious code, and God was powerful enough to demand obedience. The Israelites needed confidence in the power of their God in the face of their enemies—if God is for us, who can be against us? The demonstration would make it clear that Moses had been chosen by God to be his prophet; only he dared go near the UFO. "Lo, I am coming to you in a thick cloud, that the people may hear when I speak with you, and may also believe you [Moses] for ever" (Exodus 19:9).

The people were warned several times not to "touch" the mountain when the UFO descended on it (Exodus 19:12; 21; 24). There were religious reasons for this commandment, for this was a holy mountain; but if there was a power display on the mountain, it might have been dangerous for anyone to be on the mountain. It is interesting that Moses was shielded from danger when coming near the UFO, although after long periods in the presence of the "thick cloud" his face developed a peculiar "glow" (Exodus 34:29–35).

A mountain shooting forth lightning, thunder, and smoke like a kiln does suggest a volcano, but one does not usually find people climbing volcanic mountains as the Bible suggests Moses did; and furthermore, one could climb to the top of every volcano in the world and never encounter a being at the top of the volcano who would dictate copy for two stone tablets containing the fundamental ethics for a world religion. Of course, many people are skeptical of this whole tradition; they suppose that Moses took advantage of this volcanic display to go up the mountain, quickly write out some commandments on a couple of stones, and then return with what he called the Commandments of God. But there is one element of the Sinai tradition which, if it is to be trusted, rules out the "volcanic" explanation of the smoke, thick cloud, and lightning. The Bible says that "the Lord came down upon Mount Sinai, to the top of the mountain" (Exodus 19:20). This noisy, thick cloud did not come up from the inside of the mountain; rather, it came from above the mountain and settled upon it. We have a description here which probably points to the same pillar of cloud and of fire of the Exodus, carrying out some kind of spectacular activity. Martin Noth argues that the "cloud" at the Red Sea and at Sinai have a common tradition,[17] and with this we agree. We believe that this common tradition was not derived from a volcano, however, but from some sort of UFO which resembles modern flying saucers. Then it makes more sense to conclude with the Bible that Moses went to the top of the mountain to converse with a being in the "cloud."

Another Sinai passage points more clearly to the "pillar of cloud" tradition. "Then Moses went up on the mountain, and the cloud covered the mountain. The glory of the Lord settled on Mount Sinai, and the cloud covered it six days; and on the seventh day he called to Moses out of the midst of the cloud. Now the appearance of the glory of the Lord was like a devouring fire on the top of the mountain in the sight of the people of Israel. And Moses entered the cloud" (Exodus 24:15–18). Moses seems to have gone aboard the UFO, at which time he received stone tablets from the being in the UFO (Exodus 24:12) and also received specifications concerning the construction of the Tabernacle (tent of worship and sacrifice) for the children of Israel. "According to all that I show you concerning the pattern of the tabernacle, and of all its furniture, so you shall make it" (Exodus 25:9). When one considers the detailed information which Moses apparently received from the being in the "cloud" (roughly Exodus chapters 20–35), it is no wonder that a considerable amount of time was required for the Sinai experience. Much time was also required to collect the materials and build the Tabernacle. Supposedly before Sinai the Israelites had almost no religious tradition at all, and after Sinai they had the fundamentals of a religion which has been practiced for over three thousand years. Once these fundamentals were established, a considerable amount of time was spent in the wilderness while these principles became operational (the Bible suggests about forty years). As soon as their faith became functional, Israel moved into Palestine, the Promised Land. When Moses came down from the mountain after receiving the first tables of stone, he broke them in anger at finding the people returning to their pagan pattern of behavior (Exodus 32:15–19). Moses eventually cut a second set of stone tables, and again "the Lord descended in the cloud" (Exodus 34:5) to meet with Moses.

Notice that as the experience with the UFO continues, it is no longer called a pillar of cloud by day and a pillar of fire by night, or even a pillar of cloud, but simply the "cloud." The abbreviated form is developed very early in the Exodus account; it is in chapter fourteen of Exodus that the Red Sea incident is described, and throughout this account the UFO is usually referred to as the "pillar of cloud and of fire," or a similar long form, but even at the sea we find the short form used once. After the UFO settled between the armies of Egypt and Israel before the parting of the sea, we read, "And there was the cloud and the darkness" (Exodus 14:20). When the Israelites followed this bright cloudlike UFO into the wilderness, "the glory of the Lord appeared in the cloud" (Exodus 16:10). Just as UFO is our abbreviation for Unidentified Flying Object, so "the cloud" is frequently the abbreviation for the pillar of cloud by day and the pillar of fire by night. As the Exodus narrative continues, a shorter form is almost always used.

Once the Tabernacle had been built, the UFO moved into a position directly above the tent. "Then the cloud covered the tent of meeting, and the glory of the Lord filled the tabernacle" (Exodus 40:34). This "cloud" served as Israel's beacon throughout the journey in the wilderness. "For throughout all their journeys the cloud of the Lord was upon the tabernacle by day, and fire was in it by night, in the sight of all the house of Israel" (Exodus 40:38). The book of Numbers is even more emphatic that this cloud dictated every move Israel made; when the cloud moved, Israel moved, and when the cloud rested, Israel made camp (Numbers 9:15–23). Scholars have been led to speculate that the pillar of cloud and fire arose out of the sacrificial tradition of the Jews. When burnt offerings were sacrificed on the altar, smoke went up from the tent, moving from earth to heaven, and thus stimulating the tradition that the "pillar of cloud" represented the presence of God. But as we have seen, it is quite late in the Exodus that the Tabernacle is built, and supposedly Moses received the information of how to build the Tabernacle from the being in the cloudlike UFO on Mount Sinai. Thus the volcano and the sacrificial-cloud explanation of the origin of the pillar of cloud both have to assume that an experience which occurred late in the Exodus was, so to speak, written back into the early Exodus tradition.

But none of these explanations—that the pillar of cloud

was smoke from a fire pot which served as a beacon, or the visual impression of a volcano, or the result of the smoke and incense of a sacrificial tradition—can account for the continuous Biblical assumption that this "cloud" contained a being with whom Moses was involved in almost day-to-day conversation. When the being in the cloud wanted to talk to Moses, the UFO seemed to descend from its position above the tent (Numbers 11:25). At one point Miriam (Moses' sister) and Aaron criticized Moses for taking a Cushite wife, and they even wondered why Moses should be the only prophet in Israel. The being in the UFO apparently overheard the discussion: "And suddenly the Lord said to Moses and to Aaron and Miriam, 'Come out, you three, to the tent of meeting.' And the three of them came out. And the Lord came down in a pillar of cloud, and stood at the door of the tent, and called Aaron and Miriam; and they both came forward. And he said, 'Hear my words: If there is a prophet among you, I the Lord make myself known to him in a vision, I speak with him in a dream. Not so with my servant Moses; he is entrusted with all my house. With him I speak mouth to mouth, clearly, and not in dark speech; and he beholds the form of the Lord. Why then were you not afraid to speak against my servant Moses?' " (Numbers 12:4–8) Miriam developed "leprosy," and Israel had to remain in camp seven days until she was cured. UFO authorities such as Coral and Jim Lorenzen have noted that people have frequently developed skin irritations after a flying-saucer contact.[18]

The destruction of the Egyptians at the Red Sea, the warning to Moses not to come near the burning bush, the warning to keep away from Mount Sinai, and the experience of Miriam all suggest that it was dangerous to get too close to this UFO. The Tent of Meeting, with the UFO hovering above it, was purposely kept outside the camp for the protection of the people; apparently it was dangerous to get too close to the "Presence" (Exodus 33:7). On one occasion we read, "And the people complained in the hearing of the Lord about their misfortunes; and when the Lord heard it, his anger was kindled, and the fire of the Lord burned among them, and consumed some outlying parts of the camp" (Numbers 11:1); only Moses' intercession saved the situation. It is not surprising that this UFO commanded the respect of the Israelites.

The passage dealing with Miriam, Aaron, and Moses is enlightening, for all three persons are recorded to have heard the voice coming from the UFO. This was not simply a subjective experience of Moses, and in fact the angel in the "cloud" underlined the fact that Moses received "direct revelation" in contrast to the fogginess of a "vision" or dream which was the usual mode of revelation for prophets. The best way for God to make himself known to man, according to this tradition, is for him to speak man to man with some chosen person. Man by nature has certain physical and psychological limitations which God seems to have taken into consideration; God might even make himself best known by coming as a man (Jesus Christ), or at least by sending representative mediators or angels to make himself known.

One may very well wonder on the basis of the Old Testament passages whether God himself was present in the cloud, or whether an angel of God was in the UFO. In the Old Testament tradition we often find ordinary men— Amos, Isaiah, and Jeremiah—speaking for God. They say, "Thus says the Lord." We never suppose that God himself is literally speaking; these men are simply mouthpieces for God. If men can serve as mouthpieces for God, then certainly angels would have the right to speak for God, as they often do in the Bible. In the New Testament we find a very important speech by Stephen, his defense before the Jews who were about to stone him to death for his Christian beliefs. In this speech Stephen gave a short summary of the whole Mosaic tradition, and he clearly stated that the Hebrew faith was "revealed" to Moses by an angel or group of angels. Stephen is recorded as having said, "Now when forty years had passed, an angel appeared to him [Moses] in the wilderness of Mount Sinai, in a flame of fire in a bush" (Acts 7:30). Stephen went on to say, "This Moses whom they refused, saying, 'Who made you a ruler and a judge?' God sent as both ruler and deliverer by the hand of the angel that appeared to him in the bush" (Acts 7:35).

Stephen here clearly implied that the same angel who appeared to Moses in the bush was also instrumental in leading Israel safely out of Egypt through the sea—the pillar of cloud and fire. What can we say about the incident of the "burning bush"? We read in the Bible that "the angel of the Lord appeared to him [Moses] in a flame of fire out of the midst of a bush; and he looked, and lo, the bush was burning, yet it was not consumed" (Exodus 3:2). Moses was out in the wilderness looking after his father-in-law's sheep, and religion seems hardly to have been on his mind when he noticed a "bush" which appeared to be on fire yet did not "burn up." This was probably as much excitement as Moses could hope to have in the course of the day; he approached the bush and must have been quite

112

shocked when a voice came to him, "Moses, Moses" (Exodus 3:4).

The text records that the angel of the Lord was in the "midst" of the bush. This word *midst* is important; the Hebrew word *bush* actually means a *thicket*, suggesting a clump of bushes, and the "angel" of the Lord was in the midst or middle of a clump of bushes. In other words, it makes sense to suggest that the angel of God in the pillar of cloud and of fire which led the Israelites through the Red Sea and the wilderness had on this occasion settled down on the ground into the midst of a clump of bushes— a thicket. The UFO in the thicket made the whole clump of bushes appear to be on fire, but apparently the thicket was not consumed by the presence of the UFO, and this combination of circumstances caught Moses' attention. Since we have already seen how Moses spoke with the being in the UFO at Mount Sinai and at the door of the Tabernacle, we should not be surprised to find a voice coming out of the thicket which called, "Moses, Moses . . . I am the God of your father, the God of Abraham, the God of Isaac, and the God of Jacob" (Exodus 3:4–6). While this voice may not surprise us now, it undoubtedly surprised Moses at the time.

Having made this observation about the way in which Moses seems to have been called, let us return to Stephen's address. Stephen continued to refer to Moses and the UFO when he said, "This is he who was in the congregation in the wilderness with the angel who spoke to him at Mount Sinai, and with our fathers; and he received living oracles to give to us" (Acts 7:38). Notice that for Stephen, and apparently in the consensus of opinion of the early Church, the angel who met Moses in the "burning thicket" was also the angel who led Israel through the sea—in the pillar of cloud and fire—and to Mount Sinai, and with whom Moses spoke in the cloud at Mount Sinai. Stephen went on to say, "Our fathers had the tent of witness in the wilderness, even as he who spoke to Moses directed him to make it, according to the pattern that he had seen" (Acts 7:44). Stephen concluded by saying, "And they killed those who announced beforehand the coming of the Righteous One, whom you have now betrayed and murdered, you who received the law as delivered by angels and did not keep it" (Acts 7:52, 53). Stephen and the New Testament authors assumed that God commissioned beings from another world to come and make directly known to the Hebrew people the religion or "living oracles" they were to obey. Jesus is reported to have said that no one "has seen the Father except him who is from God; he has seen the Father" (John 6:46), which seems to imply that no one other than Jesus himself had ever seen God.

It seems quite fantastic to suggest that beings from another world came and deliberately carried out the sort of activity which is ascribed to the pillar of cloud and of fire. But if beings from another world came to earth with the intention of molding a specific religious perspective on a group of people—chosen people, the Jews—and if these beings in their UFO caused the parting of the Red Sea, provided manna in the wilderness, put on a display of power at Mount Sinai while giving Moses various instructions, and finally led Israel through the wilderness to the Promised Land, hovering night and day over the Tent of Meeting, then I dare say that the people involved in this sequence, the people who were under the influence of the beings in the UFO, might very well record the events in which they were involved. And if they were specifically told by the beings in the UFO that they should react in a religious way to these events, they might be inclined to do so. In brief, the Mosaic tradition is best explained as the visible effect caused by the UFO recorded to have been in the situation, a UFO under intelligent control. Beings from another world deliberately attempted—and succeeded—in molding a people committed to a particular religious tradition.

What happened to the UFO which led the Israelites out of Egypt through the wilderness to the Promised Land? The answer to this question is not clear. After Moses died, the leadership was turned over to Joshua, who was more a general than a prophet. Nevertheless the Lord, or the angel of the Lord, promised Joshua, "No man shall be able to stand before you all the days of your life; as I was with Moses, so I will be with you" (Joshua 1:5). Israel seems to have moved from Egypt through the wilderness of Sinai south of Palestine, marching below the Dead Sea before turning north along the eastern shore of that sea until they were some distance above the point where the Jordan emptied into the "Salt Sea," or the Dead Sea. Thus it was Joshua's task to lead Israel across the Jordan, from the eastern shore to the west into the territory of Jericho, the first city to be taken. Joshua seems to have been permitted to remain in the presence of the pillar of cloud even as a young man, while Moses was still in charge (Exodus 33:11). Many of the Biblical texts imply that the UFO continued with Israel throughout the wilderness journey (Exodus 23:20; 32:34; 33:2; Numbers 9:15–23), and it is entirely possible that the UFO led Israel to the eastern bank of the Jordan, at which time Joshua took over. There seems to have been a continuation of contact between Joshua and the Lord, as there had been between Moses and the Lord.

The Bible suggests that Israel crossed the Jordan during a flood, and it was apparently necessary to stop the flow of the river in order to make the crossing possible. The priests bearing the Ark of the Covenant moved ahead of Israel and stepped into the river, as the Lord had commanded, and as soon as the priests were in the Jordan "the waters coming down from above stood and rose up in a heap far off, at Adam, the city that is beside Zarethan, and those flowing down toward the sea of the Arabah, the Salt Sea, were wholly cut off; and the people passed over opposite Jericho" (Joshua 3:16). The "natural" explanation of this crossing is that a landslide stopped the flow of the Jordan; but again the Biblical text is very clear, with all its elaborate preparation, ceremony, and precision timing, that the Hebrews believed that the stopping of the Jordan was not an accident of nature, but rather an act of the Lord, or the angel of the Lord. If the pillar of cloud was still leading Israel at this time, it would be appropriate that the cloud should move over the river at the same time as the Ark of the Covenant moved over the river, since throughout the journey the UFO had hovered over the tent which housed the Ark. The text records that the "waters coming down from above stood and rose up in a heap far off" (Joshua 3:16).

This is precisely the description of the experience of the Hebrews at the Red Sea, except that with that sea there were two walls, or two "heaps"; since the Jordan was flowing, rather than a standing body of water like the Red Sea, only one "wall" was needed to protect Israel. The anti-G beam could very well account for this phenomenon, as in the case of the Red Sea, although the UFO is not specifically mentioned. The fact that the "heap" was far off may not so much mean that the Israelites did not see what was happening; rather, the geography of the Jordan may have dictated the place where the water could be dammed up. The banks may have been fairly low at the point of the crossing for the sake of convenience. When the Jordan was backed up, high banks would be needed to contain the water as it rose in height, and perhaps such banks could be found near the city Adam. Men would not be likely to build a city in an area where the low banks of the Jordan permitted flooding. Joshua told the Israelites that the cause behind the parting of the Red Sea and the stopping of the Jordan was the same. He said, "For the Lord your God dried up the waters of the Jordan for you until you passed over, as the Lord your God did to the Red Sea, which he dried up for us until we passed over" (Joshua 4:23). It is certainly in line with Biblical thought to say that the Lord "in the pillar of cloud" caused the parting of the Red Sea and "heaped" the waters of the Jordan by the same means. The Bible records no landslide. It probably would have if there had been one.

Once Israel successfully crossed the Jordan, the people celebrated the Passover, eating of the fruits of the Promised Land. "And the manna ceased on the morrow, when they ate of the produce of the land" (Joshua 5:12). This is another indication, together with the stopping of the Jordan, that the UFO was still present. How long the UFO remained after the crossing is not clear. Soon after the crossing "a man stood before him [Joshua] with his drawn

117

sword in his hand" who claimed to be the "commander of the army of the Lord" (Joshua 5:13, 14). Joshua was ordered to take off his shoes, for he, like Moses (Exodus 3:5), was standing on holy ground. Apparently the commander or "angel" came to instruct Joshua concerning the military task which lay ahead of him. Jericho fell by an unusual series of events. The army of Israel, preceded by the Ark of the Covenant, marched around the city of Jericho for a week, and finally, at the order of Joshua, everyone shouted and "the wall fell down flat" (Joshua 6:20). On another occasion the sun appeared to stand still for a whole day while Israel fought (Joshua 10:12–14).

Whether the pillar of cloud had anything to do with these events is not clear, although they would perhaps be easier to understand if some external agent were in the situation. It is clear, however, that after the Jordan was crossed and the manna ceased, Israel was more and more on its own. The army had to fight many fierce battles and often had to pay a high price in blood. Its battles were not always successful or decisive. However long the UFO or the "angel of the Lord" may have remained with Joshua, the Bible suggests that because of Israel's disobedience, the angel finally said, "I will not drive them [Israel's enemies] out before you; but they shall become adversaries to you" (Judges 2:3). The implication here is that the angel of the Lord departed from Israel about the time of Joshua's death (Judges 2:8). It is quite likely that if the pillar of cloud accompanied the Israelites across the Jordan into Palestine, it did not remain constantly with Israel after this period, and it may be that the UFO did not provide explicit leadership for Israel within a few days, or at most a few years, after crossing into Palestine. In the Promised

Land a new era began for the Hebrews. While they did have prophets who had visions, there seems never to have been a prophet who compared with Moses. Elijah was perhaps second in line to Moses, and there is some UFO material in connection with Elijah which is worth mentioning.

When Elijah had apparently finished his life on earth, we read that "the Lord was about to take Elijah up to heaven by a whirlwind" (II Kings 2:1). Elisha, who was Elijah's successor, was apparently with Elijah as the latter was taken away. The two men were walking together, "And as they still went on and talked, behold, a chariot of fire and horses of fire separated the two of them. And Elijah went up by a whirlwind into heaven" (II Kings 2:11). Moses and Elijah were separated by history, so that we need not expect this brief encounter with a UFO to have brought forth an immediate "pillar of cloud" response from the person who seems to have been the lone witness, Elisha. One gains the impression that it was customary for Elijah to disappear in some sort of UFO, for Elisha's fellow prophets ordered a search for Elijah; "it may be," they said, "that the Spirit of the Lord has caught him up and cast him upon some mountain or into some valley" (II Kings 2:16; see also I Kings 18:12).

One other interesting aspect of the departure of Elijah in some sort of UFO is the fact that Elijah and Elisha apparently crossed the Jordan to meet the heavenly whirlwind or chariot. There were fifty men watching at a distance as Elijah and Elisha stood next to the river. "Then Elijah took his mantle, and rolled it up, and struck the water, and the water was parted to the one side and to the other, till the two of them could go over on dry ground" (II Kings 2:8). Immediately after the crossing the UFO

119

appeared and Elijah was taken away, and Elisha took up the mantle which Elijah had left behind, and "went back and stood on the bank of the Jordan. Then he took the mantle of Elijah that had fallen from him, and struck the water, saying, 'Where is the Lord, the God of Elijah?' And when he had struck the water, the water was parted to the one side and to the other; and Elisha went over" (II Kings 2:13, 14). The fifty men on the opposite shore apparently witnessed Elisha's return and concluded, "The spirit of Elijah rests on Elisha" (II Kings 2:15). There is no explanation immediately available as to why the Jordan stood in a single "heap" for Joshua, whereas it parted in much the same manner as the Red Sea parted for Moses in the case of Elijah and Elisha. Perhaps the river was flowing slowly, or perhaps the men crossed in an area of the Jordan which formed a basin. But in each of the four cases a UFO was probably in the vicinity of the parting or stopping of the water, although in the case of Joshua this conclusion is drawn mainly by implication of the whole Exodus program. In each case, however, the event was a sign of the delegated authority of the prophet involved.

Elijah was in close contact with some force from another world. He held a contest on Mount Carmel between Baal and God, and fire fell on Elijah's offering and consumed it (I Kings 18:38); like the Red Sea incident, this was not understood by the Hebrews as an accident of nature. Baal was really the Nature God; it would be ironic to explain Elijah's success as an accident of nature! After the contest Elijah had to run for his life, and he ran to hide in a cave in the hills of Mount Horeb—where Moses first met the angel of God. While Elijah was in the cave, "the Lord passed by, and a great and strong wind rent the mountains, and broke in pieces the rocks before the Lord, but the Lord was not in the wind; and after the wind an earthquake, but the Lord was not in the earthquake; and after the earthquake a fire, but the Lord was not in the fire; and after the fire a still small voice. And when Elijah heard it, he wrapped his face in his mantle and went out and stood at the entrance of the cave. And behold, there came a voice to him, and said, 'What are you doing here, Elijah?'" (I Kings 19:11–13). Although the text does not specifically state that a "cloud" was hovering outside the cave, the indications that a UFO was present are strong. The antigravitational pressure which was evident at the Red Sea and at Mount Sinai again caused some physical consequences, including quite a gust of wind due to the downdraft, and the anti-G beam also displaced some rocks, causing a bit of a landslide and perhaps an earthquake effect. After the dust and rocks had settled down, Elijah, like Moses, heard a voice. Elijah covered his face to shield himself from the brightness of the UFO as he moved out to the entrance of the cave.

It is important to notice that the "cloud" tradition made some impression on later Hebrew literature. In the Psalms we find that the "pillar of cloud" is seen as a vehicle by which God travels—it is not God himself; "lift up a song to him who rides upon the clouds" (Psalm 68:4). It is this same God who "makest the clouds thy chariot" (Psalm 104:3); here is a possible link between the "cloud" tradition of Moses and the "chariot" tradition of Elijah. While the language is figurative, its origin in Hebrew tradition seems to be concrete. When Jeremiah wishes to speak about the mobility of God, he says, "Behold, he comes up like clouds, his chariots like the whirlwind; his horses are swifter than eagles—woe to us, for we are ruined" (Jeremiah 4:13).

A discussion of UFOs in the Old Testament usually includes an evaluation of the vision of Ezekiel, who saw UFOs which resembled "wheels" (Ezekiel 1:1–28). This vision does fit in very well with descriptions of flying saucers, but Ezekiel's experiences are different from the pillar of cloud tradition in that he alone seems to have had the vision. Ezekiel's vision was not so fundamental to the Hebrew faith as the work of Moses, although it may have been a valid prophetic experience. It seems quite logical to suppose that if beings in UFOs spent forty years developing the Hebrew community of faith, appointed prophets would quite likely have occasional contact with the angels of God. But the Biblical faith could have survived without Ezekiel's vision of "wheels"; without the "pillar of cloud" of Moses there would have been no Biblical religion.

We have not exhausted the activities of UFOs in the Old Testament; it is worthwhile to compare the visions of Isaiah 6 and Ezekiel 1. We have attempted only to show that in our present theological and scientific situation certain facts cannot be ignored. (1) There would never have been any Old Testament religion without the Mosaic tradition—the Pentateuch. (2) The acts of God in the "pillar of cloud" were fundamental in bringing about the Pentateuch. (3) This importance is summarized many times in later Biblical books as in Nehemiah 9:9–25. (4) Not only does this "pillar of cloud and fire" apparently resemble modern UFOs, and perhaps flying saucers, but this UFO is associated with the "angels" of God, men or beings from another world. If the Mosaic tradition accurately describes events which happened in history, and if flying saucers exist, then I think we can be fairly certain that beings in a UFO quite similar to—if not identical to—flying saucers were the immediate cause behind the Old Testament religion. This proves neither that God was working in the Old Testament nor that he was not working in the Old Testament. We have shown only that many of the fantastic things reported in the Old Testament apparently happened in much the way as the Bible has reported them. The Old Testament may have a fairly high degree of scientific accuracy.

Two other observations may be helpful in closing this chapter. First, we have attempted to separate dreams and psychic visions from visual Biblical UFO reports. But we cannot be sure that any civilization capable of operating the "pillar of cloud" would not also be capable of inducing psychic visions through some extrasensory technique. A total understanding of the Old Testament may require a radical union of psychology and physics. Our attempted separation between the psychic and physical may be arbitrary at several points.

Second, it should be noticed that eventually the Temple of Solomon replaced the Tabernacle of Moses as the Hebrew center of worship. The "glory" and "cloud" of the Lord also hovered over the Temple on occasion (I Kings 8:10,11; II Chronicles 7:1–3), and the Temple then became the locus of UFO visitations to priests and prophets as in Isaiah 6. It was therefore fitting for Luke to begin his New Testament Gospel with the story of how the angel Gabriel appeared to the priest Zacharias in the Temple to announce the future birth of his son John the Baptist (Luke 1:5–23).

123

CHAPTER IV

THE NEW
TESTAMENT AND
FLYING SAUCERS

Let us take as a starting assumption the possibility that the same beings who were instrumental in bringing about the Mosaic Old Testament tradition, and who also met with Old Testament prophets, were also the efficient cause behind the New Testament religion. The question then immediately arises, Who was Jesus Christ? Our temporary answer will be that, as the Christmas carol "O Come, All Ye Faithful" suggests, Christ was "born the King of Angels" (cf. Hebrews 1:4). Rather than begin with the chronological sequence of events related to the New Testament faith, let us begin by examining one of the most obvious links between Christ and the Old Testament "pillar of cloud and of fire."

THE BRIGHT CLOUD AND THE
TRANSFIGURATION OF CHRIST

The New Testament Gospels report that a short time before Christ was to be crucified, Jesus, Peter, James, and John went up to a high mountain apart from the other disciples. Jesus "was transfigured before them, and his face shone like the sun, and his garments became white as light. And behold, there appeared to them Moses and Elijah, talking with him. And Peter said to Jesus, 'Lord, it is well that we are here; if you wish, I will make three booths here, one for you and one for Moses and one for Elijah.' He was still speaking, when lo, a bright cloud overshadowed them, and a voice from the cloud said, 'This is my beloved Son, with whom I am well pleased; listen to him.' When the disciples heard this, they fell on their faces, and were filled with awe. But Jesus came and touched them, saying, 'Rise, and have no fear.' And when they lifted up their eyes, they saw no one but Jesus only" (Matthew 17:1–8).

The Church has always wondered about the significance of the Transfiguration passages in the New Testament. If one assumes that the early Christians deliberately sought to deceive people into thinking that Jesus was the chosen one, then one might expect the disciples to "manufacture" a story such as this to make an apparent link between Jesus, Moses, and Elijah. Thus, as in any case involving the reporting of news events, we are at the mercy of the reporter or witnesses. The Transfiguration was witnessed by fewer people than saw the Red Sea incident, but there were enough people there to remember the important aspects of the event in some detail. What we shall find throughout the New Testament is that the spectacular events such as the Transfiguration and the Resurrection are not performed in public view. Unlike the UFO leading Israel through the Red Sea, or the demonstration at Mount Sinai, or the showering of "bread from heaven," power in the New Testament is always undercover. While there is an underlying suggestion of power throughout the whole New Testament, the power is played down, and we shall discuss the significance of this fact more completely when we mention the "temptations" of Jesus.

Let us suppose that the Transfiguration story is an essentially valid reporting of news as we have found it in Matthew's Gospel. It is consistent exegetically and logically to believe that the "bright cloud" which overshadowed the disciples and Jesus was the same type of UFO which led Israel out of Egypt and through the wilderness—exegetically because of the parallel between the description of the bright cloud and the pillar of cloud and fire and because of the reported presence of Moses and Elijah; logically because how many beings from how many other worlds would be likely to come to earth in UFOs to set up a religion among the Jews? A voice came from the UFO, just as Moses heard a voice coming from the middle of the "thicket" which (due to the presence of the UFO in its midst) appeared to be on fire; Moses was in constant vocal contact with a being in the UFO throughout the wilderness journey. Elijah heard a voice coming to him from outside a cave, and probably the same type of UFO was present in each case.

The fact that Moses and Elijah were supposedly present at the Transfiguration obviously points to the unity between the Old and the New Testaments, as does the presence of the UFO. Whether or not Jesus was associated

127

with—indeed sent by—the God of the Old Testament is of course the most important question which could confront any Jew—and the disciples were Jews. If we find the description of the Transfiguration hard to believe, then it must be even harder to believe that Moses and Elijah were present. They had been dead for hundreds of years (except, of course, that Elijah never died on earth—he was reportedly taken away in a UFO). Besides, how could the disciples know that they had seen Moses and Elijah? My only answer to this question is that Jesus told the disciples that they had seen Moses and Elijah. (The "introductions" that must have been involved stagger the imagination. Try to imagine Jesus saying, "Peter, James, and John, I would like you to meet Moses and Elijah.")

The only way we can accept the Transfiguration sequence is to accept not only a belief in angels, an assumption on which this book is based, but also the Biblical idea of the "resurrection of the body." The New Testament does not believe simply in the salvation of a man's "soul," but preaches the resurrection of the body—based on the bodily Resurrection of Christ. The New Testament maintains that there is an angel world and that these angels, at least some of them, are special servants of God, sent to help plant the seed of the Hebrew-Christian religion in the soil of the earth—in the minds of men. The New Testament suggests that all men who accept the salvation offered in Christ will someday be raised from the dead as Christ was raised. After Christ was raised from the dead, he "ascended into heaven"; that is, he returned to the angel world from which he had come. We too, so argues the New Testament, at some point in time after we die will be taken to the angel world or the resurrection world to be with Christ (exactly *when* this will happen is a bit of a problem).

The ideas of the resurrection of the body and of angels are intimately related. I doubt that a person can believe strongly in one and not in the other. The Apostle Paul was on trial before the Jews, and he brought up the subject of the resurrection of the body to divide the Pharisees and the Sadducees because, as Luke notes in the book of Acts, "the Sadducees say that there is no resurrection, nor angel, nor spirit; but the Pharisees acknowledge them all" (Acts 23:8). Roughly speaking, one might say that Bishop Robinson and the "demythologizers" are arguing like Sadducees, and I am arguing like a Pharisee—I am suggesting belief in another world, a resurrection world, a world of angels.

Jesus himself sided with the position of the Pharisees against the Sadducees on the question of the resurrection. While on many other occasions Jesus condemned the Pharisees for their religious snobbery, he did support their resurrection theology. On one occasion the Sadducees gave Jesus a hypothetical situation in which a man died, having no children, and by custom his younger brother married the widow. There were seven brothers, and each in turn married the widow and died, leaving her to the next brother. The question was then directed to Jesus, "In the resurrection, therefore, to which of the seven will she be wife? For they all had her" (Matthew 22:28).

Jesus gave two answers to this query. First he said, "You are wrong, because you know neither the scriptures nor the power of God. For in the resurrection they neither marry nor are given in marriage, but are like angels in heaven" (Matthew 22:29, 30). Jesus takes the idea of the resurrection for granted; he knows both the Scriptures and the power of God, and both testify to the resurrection. His comment that in the resurrection men become like angels illustrates why it is nearly impossible to believe in the Biblical idea of bodily resurrection and not to believe in angels.

How do the Scriptures testify to the resurrection? Jesus continued, "And as for the resurrection of the dead, have you not read what was said to you by God, 'I am the God of Abraham, and the God of Isaac, and the God of Jacob?' He is not God of the dead, but of the living" (Matthew 22:31–32). To the astonishment of everyone, Jesus had suggested that even now Abraham, Isaac, and Jacob were alive. On one occasion Jesus said, "Your father Abraham rejoiced that he was to see my day; he saw it and was glad" (John 8:56). Jesus seems to be consciously aware of another world—a world of angels, and of persons who long ago died on earth but now live in a resurrection world. In this context we must evaluate the suggestion in the Transfiguration story that Moses and Elijah were present. What about angels and the resurrection? At this point we can only ask the question.

The Transfiguration story also suggests that Jesus was transfigured; that is, that his face seemed to glow and his garments became luminescent. Again there is a connection between Moses' experience with his UFO, for we read in Exodus that when Moses came down from Mount Sinai after conversing with the being in the UFO, "the skin of his face shone" (Exodus 34:29). Peter's response suggesting that three "booths" be made seems to imply that a holy place of worship should be set up—like the Tent of Meeting in which Moses served, with the UFO hovering over it night and day.

In the face of this experience, especially when the UFO (bright cloud) appeared, the disciples fell on their faces, perhaps out of fear, or to shield their eyes from the bright light. Then Jesus touched them and told them to get up and not be afraid. I am sorry that the disciples buried their faces, for I suspect that they would have reported seeing Moses and Elijah enter this UFO which had recently arrived and depart by means of it. As it is, the Bible says only that when the disciples again had the courage to look, they saw Jesus alone. Moses, Elijah, and the bright cloud had disappeared.

What was the purpose of this meeting at the Mount of Transfiguration? Matthew's Gospel goes on to say that "as they were coming down the mountain, Jesus commanded them, 'Tell no one the vision, until the Son of man is raised from the dead'" (Matthew 17:9). Luke's version of the Transfiguration suggests that Moses and Elijah spoke to Jesus "of his departure, which he was to accomplish at Jerusalem" (Luke 9:31). As we shall soon see, angels seemed to have played an important role in the Resurrection of Christ.

What is the significance of the Transfiguration from a philosophical point of view? The Petrine literature attributes the following words to the Apostle Peter, who is reflecting on the significance of the Transfiguration: "For we did not follow cleverly devised myths when we made known to you the power and coming of our Lord Jesus Christ, but we were eyewitnesses of his majesty. For when he received honor and glory from God the Father and the voice was borne to him by the Majestic Glory, 'This is my beloved Son, with whom I am well pleased,' we heard this voice borne from heaven, for we were with him on the holy mountain" (II Peter 1:16–18). The term *Majestic Glory* is a unique reference to the "bright cloud" type of UFO which was reported to have been present at the Transfiguration. But what we wish to point out is that it seems quite clear that the early Church considered the Transfiguration to have been a historical event, and Peter, James, and John were eyewitnesses to this event, including the presence of the UFO. Most of the "honest to God" and "death of God" theologians would argue that the UFO reported to have been present at the Transfiguration was mythological. But the above passage in II Peter stresses that the disciples "did not follow cleverly devised myths" in presenting their version of the gospel; rather, what they preached was an *eyewitness* account of the events which surrounded Christ.

Many modern theologians argue that when the Biblical people reported contact with beings from another world, this report must be interpreted as mythological in nature. But it is quite clear that in the mind of the early Church the Transfiguration passage, including the presence of the UFO, which is recorded in the Gospels (written earlier than II Peter), is not a *myth*, but an *eyewitness* account. The early Church seemed to claim to know the difference between fancy and fact as surely as do Bultmann, Robinson, or Altizer. Is the early Church to be trusted in regard to this claim? Is the Transfiguration report essentially mythological or scientific in nature? Throughout both the Old and the New Testaments there is a constant warning against idolatry. There is an awareness that men are always tempted to create a wooden God with their own hands, or a mythological God with their own minds. But the Bible claims that the God who shows himself to the

Biblical people is not one they have made with their own hands or minds—through beings from another world God has acted on the Biblical people. If the "pillar of cloud" in the Old Testament or the "bright cloud" at the Transfiguration is mythological, then it would seem that the Biblical people are guilty of idolatry, according to their own standards of judgment.

The "Glory" of the Lord and the Birth of Christ

There are various aspects connected with the birth of Christ which have tempted scholars to point to mythological origins of the traditional accounts of this event, but the idea of beings from another world operating in UFOs with the specific intention of bringing attention to the birth of Christ can certainly explain the Biblical account. What is clear in Luke's account is that the birth of John the Baptist and the birth of Jesus were both preceded by angelic visitations—Mary being visited by the angel Gabriel (Luke 1:26), who told her that she would not conceive in the usual manner, but rather by the Holy Spirit. The Bible suggests that Mary was "greatly troubled" (Luke 1:29) by Gabriel's visit, which one can well imagine.

When Christ was born in Bethlehem, angels appeared to shepherds during the night to announce Christ's birth. "And an angel of the Lord appeared to them, and the glory of the Lord shone around them, and they were filled with fear" (Luke 2:9). We saw in the book of Exodus that the pillar of cloud and of fire produced the idea of the "glory" of God, and the UFO which led Moses was called the "angel of God." It is not clear in this passage in Luke whether the shepherds actually saw angelic persons or whether they simply saw a glowing object over their heads and heard voices coming from it. Whatever the case, this sequence in relation to the shepherds is consistent with the UFO activity in relation to Moses during the Exodus and also with the UFO which we met at the Transfiguration. Matthew records that "wise men from the East" followed what they thought was a star to the place of Christ's birth. These men were undoubtedly interested in astrology, and perhaps they were following a star. The Bible says, however, that the Wise Men followed the star "till it came to rest over the place where the child was" (Matthew 2:9). But stars do not move in this manner, nor do they move and then suddenly stop. The Air Force is forever explaining to people that when they think they have seen a UFO, they have in fact seen a star or a planet; perhaps the Wise Men were involved in a reverse experience. (The Air Force would probably argue that the Wise Men were wise—and they knew a star when they saw one.) In any case, if beings from another world deliberately sought to draw attention to the birth of Christ, a space vehicle answering the description of modern UFOs would have been capable of carrying out the activities which the Bible describes: transporting beings from another world to instruct shepherds, lead Wise Men with some type of starlike beacon, or even bring Gabriel to meet Mary.

THE SPIRIT "DESCENDING" LIKE A DOVE— THE BAPTISM OF JESUS

Luke suggests that very early in his life Jesus was conscious of who he was; at the age of twelve he was arguing with Jewish teachers in the Temple (Luke 2:41–51). The Gospel of John reports that Mary, the mother of Jesus, knew that he had unusual powers and apparently encouraged him to do something about the lack of wine at a marriage feast. Although Jesus pointed out, "My hour has not yet come" (John 2:4), he nevertheless proceeded to change water into wine. Mark implies that the hour of Jesus did "come" when Jesus was baptized in the Jordan by John. All four Gospels refer to the baptism of Jesus, and scholars agree that the four Gospel accounts of Jesus' baptism share a common tradition. Although none of the Gospel writers (except perhaps John) seems to have been a witness of the baptism, each concluded that the baptism was such a crucial event in the life of Christ that each has included the baptism in his narrative.

Jesus came to John the Baptist, who had been preaching repentance from sin and baptizing in the Jordan as a sign of God's cleansing. John was hesitant to baptize Jesus, but finally consented. "And when Jesus was baptized, he went up immediately from the water, and behold, the heavens were opened and he saw the Spirit of God descending like a dove, and alighting on him; and lo, a voice from heaven, saying, 'This is my beloved Son, with whom I am well pleased.' Then Jesus was led up by the Spirit into the wilderness to be tempted by the devil" (Matthew 3:16–4:1).

After Jesus was baptized, some sort of UFO apparently entered the situation for some reason. What did the UFO look like, and what was its mission? The question as to the physical shape of the UFO has been the cause of controversy in the field of Biblical scholarship. C. K. Barrett, in his work *The Holy Spirit and the Gospel Tradition*, points to all the difficulties in saying that the UFO had the physi-

135

cal shape of a "dove" or pigeon,[1] which of course has been the assumption of the Church throughout the ages. Artists, when they wish to symbolize the Holy Spirit, have invariably painted a picture of a white dove in flight. Matthew, Mark, and John say in effect that Christ saw the Spirit "descending like a dove." The fourth Gospel says that John the Baptist "saw the Spirit descend as a dove from heaven, and it remained on him" (John 1:32). This is important, for the Biblical witness as a whole suggests that the "Spirit" was some concrete reality which anyone who happened to be present at the baptism might have seen. Luke underlines the concreteness of the Spirit by saying that it descended in "bodily" form (Luke 3:22). The UFO which descended was more than an "inner vision."

The difficulty is that Luke, in trying to stress that the Spirit in this instance was a concrete visible reality (which in Biblical thinking it usually is not), said that "the Holy Spirit descended upon him [Jesus] in bodily form, as a dove" (Luke 3:22). Here Luke seems to imply that the Spirit had the bodily shape of a dove. Nowhere else in the Scriptures—neither in the Old nor in the New Testament —is there any clear reference to the Spirit of God's looking like a dove. Before dealing with the problem of Luke's reading, it is important to remember that Luke did not say that a dove descended on Jesus; Luke said that the Spirit descended on Jesus, and the Spirit took a bodily shape which was "like" a dove. Stress the idea of likeness; a dove did not descend on Jesus—something *like* a dove did.

One of the difficulties with the "dove" concept is that the Luke reading has been made normative for the Matthew, Mark, and John readings. The latter say that the Spirit was "descending like a dove." They do not say that the Spirit physically looked like a dove—they are referring to the similarity between the way in which a dove descends in flight, wings spread and motionless, and the way in which the Spirit appears when it descends. Apparently there is nothing visibly in motion when the Spirit is seen to descend, except the motion of the whole "Spirit body," whatever that may be; the Spirit is also by implication nearly silent in its descent.

Matthew was trying to convince Jewish readers of his Gospel that Jesus was the new Moses. Therefore, any way in which Matthew could point to a link between Jesus and Moses was to Matthew's advantage. Baptism was a sign that man had been set free from sin, just as the Hebrews had been set free from slavery in Egypt. The great event which separated the Hebrews from slavery was the parting of the Red Sea; thereafter the Jews were free from Egypt. When the River Jordan stood in a "heap" for Joshua, the Israelites crossed into the Promised Land. For the Hebrews, crossing a body of water set them free from their sinful past and set them toward a new future. But also after the sea the Hebrews were led by the pillar of cloud and fire into the wilderness for a time of *testing*, and the Israelites did not stand up to the test very well—they cried for food and water, and Moses used his powers (through the UFO) to supply the needs of the people. Immediately after Jesus was baptized, Matthew tells us that "Jesus was led up by the Spirit into the wilderness to be tempted by the devil" (Matthew 4:1). Among other things Jesus was tempted to turn stones to bread to satisfy his hunger. Matthew suggests that Jesus was in the wilderness forty days and forty nights, as the Hebrews were in the wilderness forty years. As Moses was led into the wilderness by the pillar of cloud, so Jesus was led into the wilderness by the "Spirit." If Matthew in trying to say that Jesus was the new Moses were to suggest that whereas Moses was led into the wilderness by "the cloud," Jesus was led into the wilderness by a pigeon or "dove," this would almost amount to saying that Jesus was a false prophet, for the dove would be a false sign. There is no Old Testament precedent for saying that the Spirit looked like a dove. If Matthew tried to convince the Jews that Jesus was led into the wilderness by a dove rather than by the "cloud," he would be defeating his own purpose.

The second alternative is to look for ways in which the idea of the "cloud" became an equivalent of the "Spirit of God" for the Old Testament writers and for subsequent New Testament thought. When Elijah was taken up into heaven by the "chariot of fire," some of the prophets went to the hills to search for Elijah, for, they said, "it may be that the Spirit of the Lord has caught him up and cast him upon some mountain" (II Kings 2:16), because this seems to have happened to Elijah frequently. By the time Elijah was Israel's prophet, the idea of the "cloud" had been transformed into the concept of "the Spirit of the Lord." In the book of Numbers we read that seventy elders were in a sense "baptized" with the spirit of prophecy: "Then the Lord came down in the cloud and spoke to him, and took some of the spirit that was upon him [Moses] and put it upon the seventy elders; and when the spirit rested upon them, they prophesied" (Numbers 11:25). Thus with Moses and Elijah there is evidence that the "reality" with which prophets had contact—the pillar of cloud and fire —came to be associated with the "Spirit of God."

John the Baptist pointed out that the baptism in which

Jesus would be involved would be twofold, of water and of spirit or fire. John had baptized with water only. Throughout the New Testament there is a strong emphasis on the need for a twofold baptism, of water and Spirit, and Jesus, speaking to Nicodemus, pointed to the need to be "born of water and the Spirit" (John 3:5). Jesus suggested that this need was so basic to Judaism that Nicodemus, a Jewish teacher, should have realized what Jesus spoke about. In John's Gospel Jesus spoke of "Spirit" as like the wind, which is, of course, more traditional. But the pillar of cloud and fire was also apparently a symbol of baptism by the Spirit. The Apostle Paul on one occasion said, "I want you to know, brethren, that our fathers were all under the cloud, and all passed through the sea, and all were baptized into Moses in the cloud and in the sea" (I Corinthians 10:1, 2). We have here a passage which points clearly to the relation between the baptism of not only Jesus but of all Christians, and the incident at the Red Sea. Even at the Red Sea the baptism was of water and Spirit, although the Israelites did not even get their feet wet! When John the Baptist said that Jesus would baptize with fire, he undoubtedly had in mind the pillar of fire, so that when John saw the Spirit descend on Jesus, he should have expected to see the pillar of cloud and of fire descend on Jesus. This may very well be what John saw.

When the Spirit descended, a voice from heaven said, "This is my beloved Son, with whom I am well pleased" (Matthew 3:17). We have already seen at the Transfiguration that a "bright cloud overshadowed" the disciples, and a voice came from the cloud saying, "This is my beloved Son, with whom I am well pleased; listen to him" (Matthew 17:5). If both the baptism and the Transfigura-

tion are events which have been described with some accuracy, then it would seem likely that the voice which
came from the UFO on each occasion came from the *same
class or type* of UFO, and that would be the "bright
cloud" or pillar of cloud and of fire variety. The baptism
was of course witnessed by an entirely different group
of people from those present at the Transfiguration, with
the exception of Jesus, so we might expect the description
of the UFO to be somewhat different.

If it was the "cloud" which led Moses through the wilderness, which was also at the Transfiguration, and which
was also present at the baptism, then the only conclusion
we can come to is that when we read that the Spirit was
"descending like a dove," the Bible means that "the pillar
of cloud and of fire was descending like a dove," or simply
that Jesus saw "the cloud descending like a dove." We
then have to ask, Is there any Biblical precedent for comparing the flight of a cloud and a dove? The sixtieth chapter of Isaiah begins by saying that "the glory of the Lord
has risen upon you" (Isaiah 60:1) and goes on to promise
that the nations of the world will be drawn to the "light"
and "brightness" hovering over Israel. The "pillar of fire"
was of course the origin of the idea of the glory and brightness of the God of Israel. This passage of promises closes
by asking the question,

> Who are these that fly like a cloud,
> and like doves to their windows?
> (Isaiah 60:8).

In the context of this passage, which is certainly difficult,
the author seems to have in mind the whole Mosaic tradition which refers to the bright cloudlike UFO which saved

Israel from Egypt in the past, and will in the future draw all nations to it. If these "clouds" carry the angels of God, then in the tradition of Hebrew parallelism, in which the idea of the first line is carried over and stressed in the second line, we have here a comparison between the way in which clouds and doves fly, and doves of course often "descend" from above to a window below. We do have here a clear Biblical precedent for comparing the way in which clouds and doves fly, and the link may be between the flight of doves and the glorious cloud, or the Spirit of the Lord. Thus for Matthew to say that the Spirit of God was descending as a dove descends has Biblical precedent, providing that we keep in mind that by the "Spirit" Matthew means the "bright cloud" of Biblical tradition. It is important to notice here that the comparison is not between the way a cloud and dove appear in physical shape, but between the way they fly.

One fact which is not clear from the baptism accounts is exactly what happened to Jesus as the UFO descended. Matthew says, "And when Jesus was baptized, he went up immediately from the water" (Matthew 3:16). The picture which Matthew portrays is that Jesus was baptized, and as soon as he was baptized, Jesus went running out onto the bank of the Jordan. Or, as Matthew says, "he went up immediately from the water." Why should Matthew stress that Jesus went up "immediately"? If Matthew does not say that Jesus ran to the shore, he does clearly suggest that no time was wasted in getting to the bank.

While the RSV says that Jesus "went up" from the water, the actual Greek word says that Jesus "ascended" from the water, and the Greek word *immediately* suggests the notion

141

of "uprightness"; Matthew almost seems to be saying that Jesus ascended uprightly or vertically from the water. Was Jesus drawn vertically from the water into the UFO, which at this time was descending from above? Matthew then goes on to say that Jesus "was led up by the Spirit into the wilderness" (Matthew 4:1). What does Matthew mean by "led up"? One might suppose that Jesus would have been "led" like Moses, but if we remember that Elijah was "caught up" by the Spirit on occasions, then we cannot be sure. Some scholars have suggested that Jesus was "snatched away" after his baptism as later the Apostle Paul was apparently "caught up" into heaven.[2]

It is worth noting that Mark says "And when he [Jesus] came up out of the water, immediately he saw . . . the Spirit descending upon him like a dove" (Mark 1:10), so that Mark places the idea of "immediacy" with the descent of the dove, rather than with Jesus' coming out of the water. But Mark does say that the Spirit "drove" Jesus into the wilderness, which implies something more violent then simply "leading." John's Gospel reports that John the Baptist saw the Spirit "descend and remain" on Jesus. This suggests that Jesus and the Spirit merged, and furthermore that John did not see them separate from each other. It certainly would not be out of line for a UFO of the type we have seen in the Old and the New Testaments to have come upon Jesus at his baptism and to have carried him bodily into the wilderness. This would certainly make an impression on anyone who saw it happen, and would help explain why the baptism is recorded in each of the four Gospels. Whether or not the UFO carried Jesus into the wilderness, it seems quite certain that the "pillar of cloud" type of UFO was seen to "descend like a dove."

In John's Gospel, shortly after the baptism sequence, Jesus called Nathanael to be a disciple, and Jesus told Nathanael that he would "see heaven opened, and the angels of God ascending and descending upon the Son of man" (John 1:51). Matthew records that after Jesus had met his temptations in the wilderness, "the devil left him, and behold, angels came and ministered to him" (Matthew 4:11). This would appear to be information which Jesus himself would have had to give to the disciples, but it is important to note the suggestion that Jesus was in frequent contact with beings from another world. One of the questions which is often asked is: How did Jesus come to understand his own mission to the world? If we suppose that a pillar of cloud type of UFO descended on Jesus at his baptism and that this UFO either led or carried Jesus into the wilderness, then we can suppose that it was during this period that Jesus formulated his mission, just as Moses made contact with the "angel of God" on Mount Sinai in order to understand his mission.

Having examined the baptism account in some detail, I shall now refer to the problem we noted earlier, that Luke said the Spirit descended on Jesus "in bodily form, as a dove" (Luke 3:22). First, one should notice that Luke alone says "in bodily form," so that it is probably Luke, rather than Matthew, Mark, or John, who stands outside the correct tradition. It is important to remember that Luke was the only Greek author of the New Testament, and perhaps he did not completely understand the "pillar of cloud" tradition behind the account of the baptism which he heard. As Luke's account was passed on to the Greek world, immediately artists started painting "doves" as a sign of the Spirit, something a good Jew would never do.

Keep in mind also that Luke says the Spirit was in bodily form "as" or "like" a dove. Luke does not say a dove descended, but rather something like a dove. If we can imagine a white circular cloudlike UFO 100 feet in diameter descending from above, perhaps a white dove with its wings spread in a nearly circular arc does portray some similarity to what the Biblical witnesses saw, and a similarity to a modern, descending flying saucer. It is not too difficult for one's imagination to compare the way a white dove descends, silently with its wings spread, and the way in which modern UFOs described by Keyhoe, Edwards, and Vallee usually move about.

Matthew was seeking to portray Jesus as the new Moses, and in this context the temptations of Jesus make interesting reading. If there was a UFO of the pillar of cloud type which led the Israelites through the Red Sea, then this represented nothing short of a sensational demonstration of power. Moses also arranged through the UFO to have bread rain from heaven, and water came from rocks at the touch of Moses' rod. The first temptation which faced a hungry Jesus was, "If you are the Son of God, command these stones to become loaves of bread" (Matthew 4:3). Again, Jesus was tempted to leap from the "pinnacle of the temple," knowing that the angels of God would save him in the sight of everyone, thus proclaiming that he was the savior (Matthew 4:5, 6). (The temptation to leap from the temple, together with the report that Jesus walked on water [Matthew 14:25], suggests that

Jesus, together with the "angels," or the beings in charge of the Red Sea incident, may have had unusual control over the forces of gravity.) Jesus was always tempted to use his power to draw attention to himself—if he is the savior, it is important that people notice him. But it is clear from the incidents of Moses with the rebellious Israelites in the wilderness that a display of *power alone does not permanently convert people.* But Jesus seems to have had power, and when necessary he used it. Thus when he met the sick, he healed them. When five thousand became hungry, he fed them. Although he did not seem too pleased about it, for the sake of his mother he changed water to wine.

Men followed Jesus after he had fed a great multitude with "five barley loaves and two fish" (John 6:9), and Jesus withdrew because the men "were about to come and take him by force to make him king" (John 6:15). When asked why he had run away, Jesus appeared despondent because men sought him not for what he taught, but "because you ate your fill of the loaves" (John 6:26). Jesus then went on to explain that he was the eternal bread from heaven. "Your fathers ate the manna in the wilderness, and they died. This is the bread which comes down from heaven, that a man may eat of it and not die. I am the living bread which came down from heaven" (John 6:49–51).

The Jews were not too impressed with this description which Jesus had offered concerning himself. "They said, 'Is not this Jesus, the son of Joseph, whose father and mother we know? How does he now say, "I have come down from heaven"?'" (John 6:42). I cannot help thinking here that Jesus is portrayed in the Bible in much the

145

same way as our modern-day "spy" stories. Jesus came from a foreign world into our world and started to gather together a small band of people who would owe their allegiance to his world (heaven). Jesus is really an "undercover agent." An "undercover" agent is a person who lives in a foreign country, or enters a foreign country, undercover, under a cover story, living under an assumed name, perhaps working as a carpenter, or a tourist agent, or an engineer—anything which will serve to cover up his true purpose, which is espionage, undermining the nation in which he is "undercover" for the sake of another nation. According to Jesus, our world really belonged to the "devil"; Jesus defeated the world of the devil, first of all by refusing to turn in his heavenly citizenship and coming over completely to this world (the temptations), and secondly, by gathering together a strong following of persons who were committed to citizenship in the eternal kingdom from which Jesus came.

Jesus came into our world under a perfect "cover" story: By means of the virgin birth Jesus was able to come from another world, but could appear to have come naturally, to be a "natural-born citizen" of this world. Obviously the cover story was very believable. When Jesus actually told the Jews that he was a "foreign spy" from heaven, they did not believe him. They said, "We know your parents, we know where you live, you have spent your whole life in this neighborhood—you must be joking to tell us you are a foreigner, from heaven." In fact, the cover story under which Jesus came into our world was so effective that even up to the present day people are debating the question, Did Jesus come from heaven? Our country—indeed, the world—has since been literally divided in its

146

loyalty, some arguing that Jesus was a man and nothing more; others, that his true citizenship was in heaven. Those who attempt to demythologize the New Testament seem to be trying to take away Jesus' heavenly citizenship. The debate is as old as Christ—and the battle is not yet over. The temptations suggest that Jesus could have used his power to put the question beyond doubt, but that he did not want his power to distract from his "words" or teachings.

Thus the baptism of Jesus, in which he made contact with beings from another world in some sort of UFO, followed by the temptations, illustrates vividly the tensions in Jesus' ministry between using the power he held over nature, and desiring men to come to him and listen to what he had to say: "Love your neighbor, and love the Lord your God, love one another as I have loved you." Some have tried to argue that Jesus was so conscious of the need to "underplay" his power that he would never perform a "miracle," and that therefore all the accounts of miracles in the New Testament are false. It appears, however, that Jesus performed his miracles not to draw attention to himself, but rather because he found a need which he could not pass by "on the other side," as did those who saw a wounded man who had fallen among thieves. What we shall see is that the UFO which led Moses never made a powerful display before a New Testament crowd as had been done at the Red Sea; but the UFO in the New Testament does appear to small groups. There seems to be in the New Testament an undercurrent of power. The angels of God, God's army, could overpower the world by force, but they have chosen rather to send in an undercover agent to undermine our trust in

147

our "worldly" government. It is not surprising that the disciples had trouble convincing the Jews that the Christ had really come. The Jews, thoroughly fed on the Mosaic tradition, expected to be knocked flat by the power of Christ when he came.

THE SPACE CLOUD AND THE ASCENSION OF CHRIST

After Christ had carried out a ministry of at least three years, he entered Jerusalem on what has been called Palm Sunday, and the following Friday was crucified. We then read in Matthew, "Now after the sabbath, toward the dawn of the first day of the week, Mary Magdalene and the other Mary went to see the sepulchre. And behold, there was a great earthquake; for an angel of the Lord descended from heaven and came and rolled back the stone, and sat upon it. His appearance was like lightning, and his raiment white as snow. And for fear of him the guards trembled and became like dead men. But the angel said to the women, 'Do not be afraid; for I know that you seek Jesus who was crucified. He is not here; for he has risen, as he said. Come, see the place where he lay. Then go quickly and tell his disciples that he has risen from the dead . . .'" (Matthew 28: 1–7). All four Gospels suggest that there were unusual persons—beings from another world—present at the empty tomb on Easter morning to explain to the individuals who came to the tomb what had happened. We have seen that at the Transfiguration Jesus was making plans concerning the Crucifixion-Resurrection event with persons from another world (Moses and Elijah) who seemed to have arrived by means of a "bright cloud" type of UFO. There was an "earthquake" associated with the arrival of the angels at the tomb, which could indicate the presence of a UFO which might by its anti-G beam cause a disturbance similar to the one reported at Mount Sinai and the one reported by Elijah outside the cave in which he was hiding. It is important to notice that the angel at the tomb is not recorded to have had wings —in fact, Biblical angels (with the exception of the cherubim and seraphim) almost never seem to have wings. If they did have wings, this would certainly be mentioned. It is only later that Christian artists, trying to discover a logical explanation of how angels could move around in space, provided these beings from another world with wings. What distinguished the angel at the empty tomb was his "brightness," a property exhibited by the body of Jesus at the Transfiguration. The angel was different from ordinary men not because he had wings, but because "his raiment" was "white as snow." He wore unusual clothing, perhaps much as our astronauts seem always to wear white clothing to reflect certain types of radiation. It is important, however, that Jesus does not seem to have carried out the Resurrection all by himself. Whether or not the angels at the tomb were actually the instruments or agents who brought Jesus back from the dead I do not know, but it is a possibility which must be considered.

Jesus made several appearances after his Resurrection, and on one occasion he appeared to at least five hundred people at one time (I Corinthians 15:6). After Jesus had made a series of Resurrection contacts over a period of time—tradition suggests forty days (Acts 1:3), something like a month perhaps—he had one final meeting with his disciples at the Mount of Olives just outside Jerusalem (Acts 1:12).

It is this last meeting between Jesus and his disciples which concludes with his Ascension. "So when they had come together, they asked him, 'Lord, will you at this time restore the kingdom to Israel?' He said to them, 'It is not for you to know times or seasons which the Father has fixed by his own authority. But you shall receive power when the Holy Spirit has come upon you; and you shall be my witnesses in Jerusalem and in all Judea and Samaria and to the end of the earth.' And when he had said this, as they were looking on, he was lifted up, and a cloud took him out of their sight. And while they were gazing into heaven as he went, behold, two men stood by them in white robes, and said, 'Men of Galilee, why do you stand looking into heaven? This Jesus, who was taken up from you into heaven, will come in the same way as you saw him go into heaven.'" (Acts 1:6–11)

Notice that the disciples were convinced that ultimately Christ would be King of the earth, and that he would be in a position to "restore the kingdom to Israel," the kingdom once held by David. Jesus does not deny that someday the kingdom will be restored—he simply tells the disciples that it is not for them to know when. The disciples believed that Christ had the power to "take over" the earth any time. The only question was, When?

Jesus commissioned his small band to be missionaries throughout the whole earth. The Gospel of John stresses the fact that Jesus thought he had been sent as a mission-ary-savior (or if you prefer, undercover agent) by his heavenly Father. In a prayer Jesus said, "As thou didst send me into the world, so I have sent them [the disciples] into the world" (John 17:18). The best single sentence summary of the Biblical mentality is in a short parable of

Jesus: "The kingdom of heaven is like leaven which a woman took and hid in three measures of meal, till it was all leaven" (Matthew 13:33). The Old Testament religion seems to have been started by beings from another world coming into the situation and "hiding" a religion among a small chosen band of primitive nomadic people—hardly a place one would look for true salvation. When Jesus came, he was born of Mary, disguised as a carpenter's son. His small band of disciples, however, saw his power, including the shocking experience of his Resurrection from the dead, and after that experience the disciples never questioned the Lordship of Jesus. Once again the leaven had been hidden in the loaf—among an unlikely small group of men. The "demythologizers" suggest that the Resurrection was a mythological construction of the disciples, but I find it much more scientific in terms of modern psychology to suggest that the Resurrection was such a factual event for the disciples that this event convinced them it would be worth their while to die for Christ—which Peter was not willing to do before the Crucifixion. The disciples did not expect to meet Jesus three days after he was dead any more than we would expect to meet a friend three days after the funeral. Jesus said to the disciples, in effect, to go into the world as we angels have come into your world; the Father has sent me; I send you; be the leaven in the world loaf.

After Jesus had commissioned his disciples to begin working like leaven in the world loaf, "as they were looking on, he was lifted up, and a cloud took him out of their sight." At this point it is difficult to be surprised that a "cloud" took Jesus up out of sight of the disciples. While Matthew reported that a "bright cloud" appeared at the

Transfiguration, both Mark (Mark 9:7) and Luke (Luke 9:34) report simply that a "cloud" overshadowed the disciples. Thus if Matthew rather than Luke had written Acts, we might have read in Acts that a "bright cloud" took Jesus from the sight of the disciples. In any case the distinction is not important, for even as far back as the book of Exodus the "pillar of cloud and fire" had been shortened to "the cloud" (Exodus 14:20).

Bishop Robinson in *Honest to God* on the very first page of his first chapter leads with his ace. "Even such an educated man of the world as St Luke can express the conviction of Christ's ascension—the conviction that he is not merely alive but reigns in the might and right of God—in the crudest terms of being 'lifted up' into heaven." [3] The ordinary person of today might look at the passage in Acts to see what Bishop Robinson was talking about, and reading that Jesus was taken away in a "cloud," and that the rest of the passage seems to be quite literal— everyone standing around watching—would be tempted to take the word *cloud* literally; everyone knows that nice white fluffy cumulus clouds do not carry people about. Any person thus taking a quick glance at the Bible would conclude, "Bishop Robinson is absolutely right! That Ascension language certainly is 'crude.'" But this cloud was no ordinary cloud. This UFO seems to have been capable of carrying Jesus off into space—I am tempted to call it a "space cloud"—but I very much suspect that the Ascension cloud was the same UFO which led the Israelites through the Red Sea, gave Moses the commandments, carried Elijah to heaven, "descended" like a dove at the baptism of Jesus, perhaps carrying him bodily into the wilderness, as he was carried away bodily at the Ascension. This was probably the same "cloud" which brought two men to meet Jesus at the Mount of Transfiguration, and probably the same type of UFO which brought angels to the shepherds at Christmas. What Robinson has not told his readers is that the Ascension story is not abnormal —it is normal for the Biblical way of thinking.

THE BRIGHT LIGHT AND THE CONVERSION OF THE APOSTLE PAUL

One of the key turning points in the history of the Church was the conversion of the Apostle Paul. Paul, then Saul, had studied theology under the brilliant Jewish teacher Gamaliel. Paul was so zealous in his support of the Jewish faith that he became in a sense a "missionary" against the Christians, their chief persecutor. Paul was apparently present at the stoning of Stephen (Acts 8:1), and he was so successful as a "chief persecutor" in Jerusalem that he was commissioned to go to Damascus to carry his talents to a new field. When Paul was converted, it was this same militant spirit which made him such an effective Christian missionary—he was willing to travel anywhere and do anything for the gospel. Not only did Paul become the greatest missionary the Church has ever had, but he is also the greatest theologian the Church has had—his training in Jewish theology made him a perfect choice to work out the implications of the Christian faith in light of the Old Testament foundation. Paul's letters form the basis of New Testament theology, together with the Gospels and the book of Acts. One can very well ask: Where would the Church be today if it had not been for the Apostle Paul? If Adolf Hitler had suddenly during

World War II turned from Nazi Germany to become an Allied General, everyone would have been greatly shocked. It was equally a shock to the Church when Paul was converted—at first no one could believe it, and many distrusted him—as we would undoubtedly have been suspicious if Hitler had suddenly been converted to the Allied cause.

How was Paul converted? Here is one account in the book of Acts. "But Saul, still breathing threats and murder against the disciples of the Lord, went to the high priest and asked him for letters to the synagogues at Damascus, so that if he found any belonging to the Way, men or women, he might bring them bound to Jerusalem. Now as he journeyed he approached Damascus, and suddenly a light from heaven flashed about him. And he fell to the ground and heard a voice saying to him, 'Saul, Saul, why do you persecute me?' And he said, 'Who are you, Lord?' And he said, 'I am Jesus, whom you are persecuting; but rise and enter the city, and you will be told what you are to do.' The men who were traveling with him stood speechless, hearing the voice but seeing no one" (Acts 9:1–7).

The conversion of Paul is recorded in two other passages in the book of Acts, and these passages do not repeat exactly what is said in the above passage. The first passage says that the men traveling with Paul heard the voice but saw no one. The second passage says, in quoting Paul, "Now those who were with me saw the light but did not hear the voice of the one who was speaking to me" (Acts 22:9). On the third occasion Paul was defending himself before King Agrippa, and he said, "At midday, O king, I saw on the way a light from heaven, brighter than the sun, shining round me and those who journeyed with me.

And when we had all fallen to the ground, I heard a voice saying to me in the Hebrew language, 'Saul, Saul, why do you persecute me?' " (Acts 26:13, 14) Thus Acts 9:7 says specifically that the men with Paul heard the voice; Acts 22:9 says that the men did not hear the voice, but that they definitely saw a bright light; Acts 26:13, 14 states that all were affected by the light and fell to the ground, and does not tell us one way or the other who besides Paul heard the voice. However one goes about reconciling the passages, the overall impression is that the men who were with Paul were stunned by the bright light, although not blinded as Paul seems to have been (Acts 22:11). The men with Paul seem also to have felt the brunt of the experience because remarks to this effect are reported in each instance; this is a good indication that Paul did not experience a purely emotional or subjective conversion. It seems most consistent with the other Biblical material to assume that the same type of "bright cloud" space vehicle which had led the Israelites through the Red Sea (and had spoken to Moses out of the middle of a glowing thicket to call him), and which spoke to Elijah outside of the cave (Elijah covered his face because of the brightness; the bushes shielded the eyes of Moses), the UFO which was the source of the voice at the Transfiguration which said, "This is my beloved Son," and which undoubtedly was the vehicle in which Christ was taken away at the Ascension, was also the UFO which hovered over Paul and his companions on the Damascus Road, and as this "bright cloud" hovered overhead, Jesus called to Saul, "Saul, Saul, why are you persecuting me?" Saul was so shocked that he asked, "Who are you, Lord?" The voice answered, "I am Jesus." It seems consistent to argue that if Jesus "ascended" in some sort of UFO, the same vehicle brought him to Paul's company on the Damascus Road.

There is no evidence for a purely "subjective" interpretation of Paul's conversion. There were psychological factors involved, of course, but to use psychology as the only category of interpretation is not only untrue to the Biblical text, but an unconvincing answer to the very pressing question: What on earth (or in heaven) could have happened to cause a Jew of Paul's convictions to change suddenly and become a Christian—a leader of those he had persecuted? The UFO thesis we have outlined is a sufficient scientific explanation providing that UFOs exist, and such an explanation is consistent with the Biblical material as a whole. It is probably a psychological shock for most Christians to think of Paul's conversion in the way I have suggested, but Protestant Christians have usually made only one requirement for the orthodoxy of their theology; that is, that it be Biblical. The UFO theory I have outlined is certainly consistent in explaining the Biblical data. Edgar J. Goodspeed has given Paul's conversion an essentially "subjective" interpretation, and I will here quote Goodspeed to illustrate the contrast between my UFO interpretation and an essentially psychological approach:

As he drew near the city, his anguish of spirit increased. Was this then really the will of God, persecution and cruelty, baptized with the holy name of religion? Must he go on implementing it against humble, earnest people whose humility and heroism rebuked his arrogance and pride? Who was this Jesus, against whom he must so bitterly crusade in the name of God? It was midday and his figure rose before the mind of Saul, reproachful and sublime. And suddenly Saul saw him in a new light, not an impostor and upstart to be condemned and persecuted but a master and leader who could deliver him from all his confusion and pain. It burst upon him with all the suddenness of a revelation, turning his world over and restoring his moral values to their rightful place. It challenged him with the clearness of an audible voice: "Saul! Saul! Why do you persecute me?" Why, why indeed was he persecuting Jesus? He should be following him.[4]

Goodspeed has no doubt found a way to "explain" the conversion of Paul in terms which will not be offensive to twentieth-century scientific thinking. While Goodspeed undoubtedly has an understanding of some of the psychological elements involved, one cannot help feeling, if the name of Jesus were pressing so hard on the mind of Saul as he approached Damascus, that when he heard the "almost" audible voice calling his name, it was hardly appropriate for Saul to answer the voice with the question, "Who are you, Lord?" The other unfortunate aspect of Goodspeed's account is that it gives one the impression that Paul so to speak converted himself by pulling himself up by the bootstraps of his own conscience. Paul writes to Timothy that God was merciful to him (Paul), appointing him an Apostle for Jesus Christ "though I formerly blasphemed and persecuted and insulted him; but I received mercy because I had acted ignorantly in unbelief" (1 Timothy 1:13). Paul finds that he is a good sign of hope for the Church; he is the chief of sinners—if he can be saved, anyone can be saved. Paul certainly believed that if God had not acted in a special way on the Damascus Road, he would have continued to persecute the Christians "in ignorance and unbelief."

Summary of the New Testament and Flying Saucers

We have pointed to five main "events" in the New Testament which certainly suggest the presence of a UFO which is sometimes described as a "bright cloud," recalling the UFO which had such close contact with Moses. There is one aspect of each of these five events which has gone almost unnoticed. The bright "glory" which shone around the shepherds at night, while the angels sang, was seen by only a few men who would hardly be called the leaders of Jewish society. The event took place out in the country away from a populated area. The baptism of Christ took place out in the wilderness by the Jordan River, and very few people were likely to see the UFO *descend* like a dove. Only Jesus, Peter, James, and John seem to have been present to witness the "bright cloud" at the Mount of Transfiguration, a mountain which again was away from a population center. Jesus was taken away from the disciples at the Ascension by a space "cloud" which was seen only by the disciples. They were apparently at the Mount of Olives at the time, outside Jerusalem. Finally, the UFO which caused the bright light to flash over the Apostle Paul and his small band of travelers on the road to Damascus was again seen in a place which was not likely to attract the attention of a city population. How unlike the "pillar of cloud and fire" which was constantly before the Hebrew people, demonstrating its power at the Red Sea. Thus in contrast to the Old Testament, while the same "beings from another world" or "forces" or "UFOs" seem to be at work in the New Testament, we never find the fantastic display of power in the New Testament that we found in the Old Testament, in front of thousands of witnesses. When power is shown, those who witness it become the "leaven" in the world loaf.

Although a scientific and theological study of the relation between flying saucers and the Bible could go into greater depths of scholarship and scientific and philosophical background than we have gone, we have examined enough of the Biblical material to show that it is quite likely—if flying saucers exist—that beings from another world in some sort of UFOs deliberately caused the Biblical religion. We have not *proved* that this is the case, but it seems quite likely—it has a fair degree of *probability*. The difficulty is that a host of questions remain unanswered. To give an example of two pressing questions: (1) What was the motive of the beings who started the Biblical religion? Did they do it just for fun, or are they under the command of the God and Lord of the Universe? (2) Where do these beings come from? If they are beings from another planet "playing games" with us, where do they come from? If they are angels from God, where is heaven?

The difficulty with each of these questions is that if we have drawn the conclusion that beings in UFOs were active in developing the Biblical religion on the basis of less than conclusive evidence, then if we are to form any answers at all to the two questions just raised, it is quite clear that from a scientific point of view such answers must be considered pure speculation. At this point science and religion begin to diverge even more.

In regard to the first question, suppose that the man of science and the man of faith could agree that the Biblical religion was deliberately caused by beings from another world who are now watching our "progress." Each man may raise the question: Are these beings simply playing games, or are they under the command of God? G. Inglefield and Jacques Vallee agree that a series of UFO appearances in Fatima, Portugal, in 1917 in connection with the Virgin Mary are apparently related to the Christian faith, and they ask this same basic question.[5] Was the event a "miracle," or a large interplanetary "hoax"? The man of science can express his opinion, "It seems more probable to me that . . . ," or he may prefer to say, "I cannot decide without further evidence." It is perfectly legitimate in the field of science to sit on the fence until more evidence is available, provided that the scientist pursues the question faithfully in each direction. But the man of faith must decide now. It seems quite clear that the Biblical people were called upon to commit themselves to Christ on the basis of the evidence they had— incomplete or otherwise. Many accepted Christ on the evidence of one miracle. Scientists might argue that one miracle does not compel one to conclude that the miracle worker was a savior. But the man of faith must decide, because the whole course of his life depends on his decision. In science a man may be compelled to find a cure for cancer because time lost is life lost. The Bible argues in effect that time lost in deciding the answer to the question "Who do you say that I am?" is life lost. So we must ask, Was Christ sincere, was he on the level in claiming to be the Son of God—was he telling the truth? On the basis of the witness of the Gospels, which is about all the evidence we have, we have to ask: Would Jesus pretend to pray to his heavenly Father; would he preach "love" while living a lie; would he even go so far as to be crucified to carry out his "hoax"? At this point the person rather than the works of Christ becomes focal.

The second question—where do these "angels" come from, a planet, or from heaven? (the two might be identical)—presents similar problems. There is little evidence for the pure scientist, but the man of faith who decides that beings in UFOs are from heaven must ask, on the basis of the Biblical witness, Where is heaven? Before describing the whereabouts of heaven, we would like to visit it. At present this presents problems; nevertheless, notice that scientists have gained much information about the moon without visiting it. They have used instruments as "mediators" between earth and the moon. By using telescopes and cameras mounted on telescopes, and by sending rockets to the moon which have televised photographs to earth, scientists have given us much knowledge of the moon. All Christians have is the Bible, which is nevertheless for the Christian in many cases a record of things said by beings from another world about their world. Jesus often spoke about the other "world" from which he had come. Thus the Bible, with its record of the words of Jesus, the angels, prophets, and apostles, becomes a "mediator" between us and heaven; the Bible is our telescope through which we look for heaven. Just as our astronauts may someday bring back to earth information about another world, so Jesus and the angels may provide us with information about their world. However unsatisfactory a record or instrument the Bible may be to some scientists, at the present time it is what the man of faith has available to him. A scientist who wishes he had more evidence nevertheless does use what evidence he has. When we move into eschatology, we move into the twilight zone of the Christian faith. But Christians have always wondered in their dreams, Where is heaven?

CHAPTER V

WHERE IS HEAVEN?

If the Biblical religion was planted and nurtured by persons from another world, it is only natural that we should wonder where these beings come from. Keyhoe, Edwards, and others who have written concerning flying saucers have suggested that the only likely explanation is that these beings come from another planet, either within or without our solar system. Bishop Robinson begins his *Honest to God* by saying, "The Bible speaks of a God 'up there.' No doubt its picture of a three-decker universe, of 'the heaven above, the earth beneath and the waters under the earth,' was once taken quite literally. No doubt also its more sophisticated writers, if pressed, would have been the first to regard this as symbolic language to represent and convey spiritual realities." [1] Bishop Robinson's chief objection to the Ascension passage in the book of Acts is that it reflects this "primitive" notion of a three-decker cosmology.

It is wise when reading the Biblical material, at least from an empirical point of view, to try to separate what the Bible reports as apparent "sense data" from the conclusions the Bible gives us about the significance of the sense data it reports. It may be that on most occasions we will want to accept both the "sensual" report and the "conclusion." Thus the Bible may report that Jesus died on the cross, and it may draw the conclusion that the blood of Christ shed on the cross saves us. We may want to accept both the "data" and the "conclusion," or we may want to accept only the data. In the case of the Red Sea incident, I accepted the data that an east wind was blowing, but I did not accept the Biblical conclusion that the wind *caused* the water to part. Bishop Robinson seems to have reasoned that since he cannot accept the Biblical conclusion that we live in a "three-decker" universe, this automatically permits him to dismiss the "sense data" which the Bible reports concerning the fact that Jesus was taken off into space by some extraordinary "cloud." The "de-mythologizers" have not made this epistemological distinction clear. It is entirely possible to admit that the Biblical cosmology was primitive without concluding that the "sense data" the Bible reports was false. We may not live in a three-decker universe, but the disciples may still have seen Christ taken off into space. After bringing up the subject of the "three-decker" universe, Bishop Robinson then admits that some writers would have regarded this as "symbolic language to represent and convey spiritual realities." What does he mean by "symbolic language" and "spiritual realities"? He means that when man starts talking about the invisible, language often becomes (of necessity) obscure. But the Bible makes it clear that many of the most important realities in the universe are invisible. Scientists who like to "see" everything may not like this, but the Bible says that is the way things are. In Colossians we read that Jesus Christ "is the [visible] image of the invisible God" (Colossians 1:15). God is invisible. Jesus taught his disciples to pray, "Our Father, who art in heaven." If God is invisible, probably heaven is invisible. How does man get to know an invisible God? First, God, though invisible, nevertheless literally is present to, and surrounds, every living being (Acts 17:28). Second, God sends his angels to the earth to make himself known, and finally reveals himself in Jesus Christ, the *visible* image of the *invisible* God. This is the basic Biblical argument. The question must now be raised: How can Jesus Christ and angels be visible on earth and invisible in heaven?

The answer which might be given by persons who believe that UFOs come from another planet is that they would be too far away to be seen. This is a possibility, but from a theological point of view it may be objectionable to suggest that heaven is on another planet. There seems to be a difference in the Bible between the "heavens" (planets, stars), which God created with the earth, and "heaven," which does not seem to be created.[2] Heaven—and hell— should be entirely different universes, as the "three-decker" universe of the Bible suggests. But our universe seems to be homogeneous. Is there any way in which a "three-decker" universe might exist in terms of modern science, in such a way that the Christian idea of angels and of the

165

resurrection of the body might be true, and still permit heaven to be invisible?

For the next two chapters we will discuss "Christian eschatology," the doctrine of the end of things—the future. It is extremely hazardous to try to explain what happened to the Apostle Paul on the road to Damascus, even with the description of the event recorded three times in Scripture. How much more difficult to discuss the possibility of how things may be in the future in a world we cannot see! All we can do is to show that many elements of Christian eschatology are not necessarily in contradiction with some aspects of modern views of space. What evidence do we have? The Resurrection of Christ is a recorded Biblical event which points to what the Apostles' Creed calls belief in "the resurrection of the body, and life everlasting." Psychologists have sometimes referred to this wishful thought of eternal life as "pie in the sky bye and bye." However unlikely this possibility may seem from a scientific point of view, if the Bible has recorded the facts correctly concerning Jesus Christ—and if he really is the Son of God—then we are faced with the possibility that the universe really works in much the way as has been outlined in Scripture. If the Bible is right, we have to look not only for "pie in the sky," but also for "heat in the deep."

One difficulty is that people have argued that heaven is not so much a place as a state. Of course this is just a guess, the basis of which seems to be that the "resurrection body" of persons will be "spiritual" rather than physical. Paul argues that we are resurrected into a "spiritual body" (I Corinthians 15:44), which suggests to some that the body is immaterial. In this same letter to the Corin-

166

thians, however, Paul was speaking about the Israelites in the wilderness who "all ate the same spiritual food and all drank the same spiritual drink" (I Corinthians 10:3, 4), although in the RSV we find that the word "supernatural" has been substituted for "spiritual" because the translators feared misunderstanding; but the translators did not speak of a "supernatural body." Paul seems to have thought that the "spiritual bread" from heaven (from the UFO) and the "spiritual body" of the resurrection were similar. Perhaps the words *heavenly body* and *heavenly bread* would better express Paul's idea—both were made of a "heavenly substance," whatever that might be. Jesus said that in the resurrection we become as angels. It is quite clear from the Resurrection appearances that Jesus did not seem to have an ordinary body. But it was a body his disciples could touch, just as angels seem to be substantial beings. In an age in which mass and energy are transferrable, perhaps this debate is not too crucial. But it seems that we can expect our resurrection bodies—if we want to trust the Biblical view of eternal life, which I do—to occupy some space somewhere. Therefore, it is appropriate to ask the question: Where is heaven?

If the first chapters in this book have *bordered* on science fiction, then the following chapters undoubtedly move almost without fear into something that reads very much like science fiction. What follows is not necessarily true, but I do believe that the next two chapters may help to set our minds free from the somewhat depressing agnosticism we now find ourselves in when we even begin to entertain the idea that we might live eternally—as part of God's plan. We have been almost too discouraged to go on looking for a sign that God really does have eternal plans for us. If the next two chapters serve to show that the Biblical idea of the future—of the resurrection of the body into some heavenly existence—may be scientifically possible, then I will feel that they have served their purpose: to set men's minds free to entertain a lively hope in the gospel.

To be consistent with the method we have employed in evaluating the Biblical material up to the present time, to ask the question "Where is heaven?" is also to ask the question, "Where do flying saucers come from?" The present consensus of most writers is that since there are perhaps millions of inhabitable planets in the universe, flying saucers probably come from one such planet, and the nearer to earth the better. A *Time* magazine essay, "A Fresh Look at Flying Saucers," points out how difficult long-distance space travel becomes. "Even the nearest star, Proxima Centauri, is 4.3 light-years away. And because presumably no spaceship—or any matter—can travel at or beyond the velocity of light, which is the universal speed limit according to the Einstein theory of relativity, it would take considerably longer than 4.3 light-years to reach the earth from its nearest stellar neighbor. At the 17,500 m.p.h. that astronauts travel, it would take nearly 170,000 years." [3]

We are still in the stone age of space travel, so that it is probably quite misleading to compare the speed of our spaceships with those of beings who are really advanced in space travel. But *Time*'s essay raises an important question: What does Einstein's theory of relativity have to do with space travel, and what sort of possibilities does the theory contain concerning our search for heaven? Although

I am no authority on relativity, I will try to examine some of the issues.

One of the basic assumptions of Einstein and Eddington and others who have developed the general "theory of relativity" is that space, time, and gravitation are interdependent, not independent.[4] In fact, gravitation came to be understood as either a property of space, or of matter which permeated and influenced all space. Thus any point particle is in effect under the influence of the whole universe. Furthermore, non-Euclidean geometry had been developed, and it was suggested that space may not be "straight" or "flat," but rather curved, and that all objects traveling in space follow a curved path.

Einstein predicted that the gravitation of the universe would even deflect light rays, and this was later experimentally verified. He was led to conclude that the universe might be "finite, but unbounded," meaning that although there is no physical boundary to the universe, the gravitational field of the universe would act as a "fence," so that any point particle traveling in space—even a ray of light— would be bent in an arc and would never escape a certain volume or area of space. Thus the force of gravitation would cause our usable space to be finite. Matter in space is something like a dog on a leash, tied to a stake. The dog can wander in a circle around the stake—his world does not appear to be bounded, but it is finite. He is limited by the leash (force of gravitation) which pulls him in toward the center stake.

Another aspect of Einstein's thinking, which has been verified to some extent by experimental observation, is that any mass which is accelerated takes on an additional apparent mass, and as the mass approaches the speed of light, this increase in apparent mass becomes greater. This is one of the reasons scientists were led to conclude that it would be impossible to accelerate any mass—including a spaceship—to a velocity which would equal or exceed the velocity of light.

Since gravity provides resistance to acceleration, we have to have rockets to send our spaceships into orbit. The rockets counteract the resisting force of gravity. As we have already pointed out, however, many of the flying-saucer reports suggest that saucer activity is so unusual that some have come to the conclusion that the beings who developed the saucers have somehow developed a technology which has set them free from the effects of gravity. Major Donald E. Keyhoe, in his book *The Flying Saucer Conspiracy*, devotes a full chapter to the idea of an antigravitational field.[5] He points out that saucers have been seen to make right-angled turns at high speeds, and to accelerate from a velocity of zero to eighteen thousand miles an hour almost instantly. Saucers have apparently on occasion caused electromagnetic interference, such as shorting out the electrical systems of automobiles. We assume that saucers have some kind of propulsion system, and yet they usually make no noise. These are some of the reasons that have led men such as Keyhoe, Edwards, and Vallee to conclude that saucers are propelled by generating some kind of antigravitational field or shield. Whether or not the term *antigravitational* is the best term to describe the phenomenon is not clear. But in any case, we have to ask the question: If the civilization behind the saucers has found a means to escape the effect of gravity, what does this mean?

170

We have mentioned that according to Einstein, our visible universe is "finite, but unbounded." Our universe is finite to us because we are bound to our universe by gravitation like a dog tethered to a stick. If we were to be set free from the effects of gravity, however, I can see no reason why we would not be free to move beyond our universe into a new space, much as if a dog had been cut free from his tether. Scientists have been discussing the possible existence of "antimatter"; there is no logical reason why only one type of matter could exist. Some material substance might exist outside our universe if it were somehow unaffected by the gravitational field of our universe. It might be possible for several universes to coexist, much as several boats sail the ocean, provided that each universe has a *different type of gravitational system* so that none are attracted toward any others. If gravity is the property of the curvature of space, it might be possible for several universes to coexist separately, provided they were governed by different spatial curvatures. But this still leaves us with the problem that since according to the relativity theory the speed of light is the universal speed limit, it would take millions of years traveling at the speed of light to reach any possible universe outside our own. Perhaps, however, since our concepts of relativity are still being explored by science, there is a yet undiscovered way to overcome this "speed limit." Then almost infinite speeds might become possible.

This is of course speculation, but I do believe the present concepts of space, cosmology, and the whole question of the nature of the universe are so open that we do have the freedom to speculate in this way; however uncertain our conclusions, we can still explore the Biblical framework without having to feel intellectually guilty about doing so. Although science has made fantastic discoveries about the universe, many of these discoveries have simply opened brand-new fields which need to be explored.

If the theory of relativity permits us to imagine heaven as a universe separate from and beyond our own universe, this is by no means the only possible solution to the problem, and I will now suggest another. Our own space may be curved, either in a negative or positive direction, or it may have a zero curvature. Scientists have not decided which type of curvature is characteristic of our own universe, but given the idea that our space is curved, it is interesting to consider concepts in mathematical space topology such as Jordan's Curve Theorem which states in effect "that there are an inside and an outside of a simple closed curve in a plane." [6] This idea seems to imply that if our universe is similar to a closed curve, then there might be an "inside" and an "outside" universe coexisting *in the same space* with our own universe. We are led to ask the question: Would it be possible for universes of different spatial curvatures to coexist in the same space? Could you move from one universe to another provided you understood the spatial curvature, or gravitational formula for each space?

This reads like science fiction, but it is interesting to examine one flying-saucer report recorded by Keyhoe. He points out that there seem to be at least two types of UFOs: the "flying-saucer" type, and a cigar-shaped "mother ship" into which flying saucers have been seen to fly. Keyhoe records this report by Captain James Howard and the crew of a BOAC air liner:

As Captain Howard was checking his arrival time, a dark object appeared a few miles to the left. Flying parallel to the plane, it was clearly visible in the light from the setting sun. Manoeuvring around this mysterious craft were several small, round objects. For a few moments Captain Howard and his co-pilot, First Officer Lee Boyd, watched in amazement. Until then Howard had been sceptical of flying-saucer reports, and Boyd had been only half convinced.

The small saucers appeared to be flying in and out of the larger ship, though the pilots could not be sure.

Suddenly the mother-ship changed its position, making it appear to change shape, just as an aeroplane, seen from different angles, assumes varying shapes.

Both Captain Howard and Boyd were convinced that the objects were solid. And from the way the six small UFO's manoeuvred, circling and apparently boarding the mother-ship, they were obviously under intelligent control.

Calling Goose Bay Air Force Base, Boyd reported the strange formation. Within seconds two U.S. Sabrejet fighters were scrambled to meet the *Centaurus*.

By now all the crew and some of the passengers had seen the saucer formation. Had this been a cargo flight, Captain Howard might have risked a closer approach. But with the lives of the crew and fifty-one passengers to consider, he decided against it.

The mother-ship and its smaller saucers were still flying parallel to the *Centaurus* when one of the Sabrejet pilots radioed the airliner from a point twenty miles away. The saucers, Captain Howard told him, were still pacing his plane.

"I'll be there in two or three minutes," the Air Force pilot answered.

Then a strange thing occurred.

Quickly the six smaller craft merged with the mother-ship. Accelerating at tremendous speed, the larger machine vanished in a matter of seconds.[7]

It is possible to conclude with Keyhoe and the pilots that the dark object was a mother ship and that it disappeared quickly because a gravity-free spaceship would have the property of extremely rapid acceleration. But given the idea of the "curvature" of space, and of an "inside" and "outside" universe, it would be possible to speculate that the so-called mother ship into which the saucers flew was in fact a bend or warp in the space-time continuum, some kind of space "tunnel" from the "middle" universe to either the "inside" or "outside" universe. One can well wonder why the saucers seemed to be bright while the mother ship was "dark." Were they made of different material, or was the mother ship in fact not a ship, not material, but rather some kind of strange void? This dark object appeared to change shape. Is this because the "mother ship" changed position as Keyhoe suggested, or might this have been the natural result of stress placed on the space "tunnel" due to the changing position of the planets in our solar system, causing a variation in the density of the gravitational field? Keyhoe reports that the mother ship appeared to accelerate very rapidly, and of course this is possible. But if the space tunnel were suddenly to close, it would probably close like a camera shutter, giving the appearance of an object moving rapidly away, and finally diminishing to a point. Thus given the idea of the curvature of space, and the fact that space and gravitation are interdependent, it is possible to conjecture that more than one universe might coexist in the same space, and if you knew how to control gravity, you might also know how to control your space and move from one spatial curvature to another.

Whether the pilots in the BOAC liner saw the saucers disappear into a mother ship, or into some sort of space tunnel leading to another invisible universe right in the midst of us, I do not know. But given the various cosmological possibilities which seem to be inherent within the general theory of relativity, I think that the idea of the space tunnel cannot be ruled out immediately on theoretical grounds. On the basis of the report recorded by Keyhoe, I believe that a space tunnel is a possible interpretation of what was observed. It is *easier*, I think, to believe Keyhoe's interpretation, that the dark object was a mother ship. But it would be a mistake at this point in our understanding of cosmology, or in our understanding of the point of origin of flying saucers, to rule out any possibility before more evidence is available.[8]

UFOs have been seen to change shape, going through something like a "folding" process, and to disappear so rapidly that they have been described as going "out like a light."[9] Since UFOs and beings associated with them apparently have unusual control over gravity (in the Bible, everything from the parting of the Red Sea, or the Jordan River, to Jesus' walking on water), and since modern science has suggested that gravitational forces may be linked with curvatures of space, we must remain flexible in regard to the problem of where UFOs originate. It is important to realize that in the past half-century concepts of space have become much more fluid, much more open than those accepted by science before 1900. It is perhaps best at this point to remain undecided about the truth value of my "space tunnel" interpretation. It does not seem too probable, but scientific concepts seem to be fluid enough that we cannot automatically rule it out. In this "undecided" frame of mind let us examine some of the Biblical concepts of the nature and location of heaven.

The "Spirit of God" and the "Opening of the Heavens"

When Jesus was baptized, he saw "the Spirit of God descending like a dove, and alighting on him" (Matthew 3:16). Where did this UFO come from, according to the Biblical account? After Jesus was baptized, "the heavens were opened" and the Spirit seems to have descended from this "opening." This idea of an "opening" represents an example of the "mythological" expression of the Biblical cosmology against which Bishop Robinson and others have written. The "opening" suggests that in our "three-decker universe" "a door" leads from our world below to the world above where the angels live in heaven. In the first chapter of Genesis we read that God created "a firmament in the midst of the waters, and let it separate the waters from the waters" (Genesis 1:6). The early Biblical people seem to have believed that there was something like a glass sheet which held water up in heaven (apparently outer space was thought to be mostly water); when rain was needed, various doors were opened in heaven to let the rain come down. Thus when the great flood came upon Noah, we read that "on that day all the fountains of the great deep burst forth, and the windows of the heavens were opened" (Genesis 7:11).

We have to admit that there is here a primitive cosmology, and certainly something like it may have prevailed during the whole Biblical period. But the idea which the "firmament" expresses may be useful, if somewhat modified, in order to understand our own relation to heaven. Our visible universe seems to be essentially homogeneous and created. It seems unlikely that no matter how far one traveled into outer space, one would find heaven. But there may be something like a "glass sheet" which separates our created universe from both "heaven" and "hell." I am suggesting that by using the concepts of the curvature of space in Einstein's universe, there may be something like a "three-decker universe." In Robinson's "three-decker universe" heaven is simply the "third story" on a house, the earth is the second story, and hell is the first (or the cellar), each stacked one on the other; this may have represented the primitive Biblical view, as Bultmann, Robinson, and others have argued. But what about a three-decker universe in which the stories are not so much vertical to each other as horizontal to each other? The universes are separated by "walls" rather than by floors and ceilings, although this analogy is not adequate, because heaven, hell, and our visible universe may in fact occupy a "one-room house," but by means of a variation in the curvature of space, whether positive, negative, or zero, we are able to have three universes occupy the same volume of space. One would perhaps move from one universe to the other by "bending space" so that an opening would be made.

Keyhoe, as we have seen in his *Flying Saucer Conspiracy,* has shown that UFOs of the saucer type have been seen to fly in and out of some dark object which we have suggested was a "space tunnel." If those present at the baptism of Jesus saw the "Spirit of God" (the bright cloud) emerge from some dark opening above, then perhaps we have here the link between our world and the next. This of course stretches scientific knowledge, proper Biblical exegesis, and the imagination to a limit which perhaps cannot be justified, but it is a useful model by which further to examine Biblical thought. One interesting fact about the use of the Greek word for *opening* is that it refers to opening places which otherwise would be closed to man.[10]

When Stephen was about to be stoned, he "gazed into heaven and saw the glory of God, and Jesus standing at the right hand of God; and he said, 'Behold, I see the heavens opened, and the Son of man standing at the right hand of God'" (Acts 7:55, 56). The reference to God's "glory" might indicate the presence of a "bright cloud" type of UFO, and we find Stephen apparently seeing in some kind of vision the "opening" or bending back of space. None of the other persons present seems to have had this vision, which shares something of the apocalyptic character of the Revelation of John. Whether the experience of Stephen was psychological, physical, a combination of both, or neither is difficult to say. But it is interesting that Stephen seems to have sensed that God was present as if he were in the "next room," so to speak. The door to the next room was momentarily opened to him.

Why did Stephen "gaze into heaven"? The passage says that Stephen, "full of the Holy Spirit, gazed into heaven" (Acts 7:55). The Holy Spirit in the Bible is usually *invisible*, but nevertheless present to each person. The Holy Spirit seems to be an invisible power from another universe which is right in the midst of our universe. At Pentecost the disciples "were all together in one place. And suddenly a sound came from heaven like the rush of a mighty wind, and it filled all the house where they were sitting. . . . And they were all filled with the Holy Spirit" (Acts 2:1–4). I will not even begin to attempt to explain what happened at Pentecost, but one gains the impression that the Holy Spirit seems to have "broken through" the space of the room where the disciples were gathered. The "breakthrough" was reported to have caused a physical disturbance, "like the rush of a mighty wind," an effect that might result from the "bending" or "opening" of space. When the Holy Spirit came upon Stephen, he did not gaze "up" to heaven; he gazed "into" heaven, as if it were in the next room. Jesus did not ascend "up" to heaven; he ascended "into" heaven, to the "inner sanctuary" of the presence of God. Perhaps the use of the preposition "into" is more important than we have realized in expressing the location of heaven.

On another occasion the Apostle Peter fell into some sort of trance, and he "saw the heaven opened, and something descending, like a great sheet, let down by four corners upon the earth. In it were all kinds of animals and reptiles and birds of the air." (Acts 10:11, 12) Peter was told that he should kill and eat the contents of the sheet-like UFO which was lowered in front of him. Peter, a Jew, had never eaten unclean food, and he was told to eat to prepare him for his meeting with the Gentile Cornelius, who had heard an angel in a vision tell him to send for Peter. Both Peter and Cornelius reacted as if they made contact with a strange world which was somehow in their midst, but was usually invisible.

179

"The Kingdom of God Is in the Midst of You"

On one occasion Jesus told his disciples, "where two or three are gathered in my name, there am I in the midst of them" (Matthew 18:20); how could Christ be present to the disciples, yet invisible? Although it is not clear what happened, Luke records that Jesus was led by the villagers of Nazareth "to the brow of the hill on which their city was built, that they might throw him down headlong. But passing through the midst of them he went away" (Luke 4:29, 30). This passage implies that Jesus passed through their midst without effort. One of the more debated passages in Scripture is the answer Jesus gave to the Pharisees concerning the coming of the kingdom of God. "Being asked by the Pharisees when the kingdom of God was coming, he answered them, 'The kingdom of God is not coming with signs to be observed; nor will they say, "Lo, here it is!" or "There!" for behold, the kingdom of God is in the midst of you'" (Luke 17:20,21).

The first question must be, What is meant by the phrase *the kingdom of God?* It must be remembered that Matthew almost never uses the phrase *the kingdom of God;* rather, he speaks of the equivalent *kingdom of heaven.* Luke, on the other hand, almost always speaks of the *kingdom of God.* The kingdom of God (or heaven) would necessarily be a place where God reigned. Would this be on earth or in heaven, or both? It is clear from the teaching of Jesus that there is a distinction between heaven and earth. In the "Lord's Prayer" we read "thy will be done, on earth as it is in heaven" (Matthew 6:10). The Jews believed that indeed someday the kingdom of heaven would come to earth, and it was this belief which motivated the question the Pharisees raised concerning the coming of the kingdom.

The answer Jesus gave can be given a number of interpretations:

The kingdom might be "in the midst of you" in the sense that God is concerned with man's heart or mind, and he seeks to come into the "midst" of the life of every person. Thus the idea of the "kingdom" is given a spiritual or mental interpretation. But this interpretation is unsatisfactory because Jesus, knowing his opinion of the Pharisees, would not have been likely to tell them that the kingdom was within *them*. One would not expect the kingdom to be found in the minds of the hypocritical Pharisees.

The generally more acceptable interpretation is that Jesus was referring to himself. He was standing "in the midst" of the Pharisees, and the kingdom of God was embodied in Jesus. When Jesus says that the kingdom is not coming with "signs to be observed," he could have been referring to the fact that in the coming of Christ the power of God was underplayed; Jesus here acknowledges his "undercover agent" role which had been defined in the scenes in the wilderness during his temptations. The kingdom was hidden in an innocent-looking carpenter's son, standing in the midst of them. John the Baptist came preaching that "the kingdom of heaven is at hand" (Matthew 3:2), which was the Biblical way of pointing to the coming of Christ. The main difficulty with saying that the kingdom was fully present in Christ is that Luke, after recording this incident with the Pharisees, moves on to describe an apocalyptic passage which Jesus relates to his disciples, and this passage speaks more directly to the question the Pharisees raised. Jesus says, "For as the lightning flashes and lights up the sky from one side to the other, so will the Son of man be in his day" (Luke 17:24). Jesus taught that some aspect of the kingdom will be consummated in the future. He suggests that the Son of Man (i.e., himself) will someday in the future return with the suddenness and brightness of lightning flashing across the sky. In the final chapter we shall deal with the "second coming of Christ," but it is important to notice that the early Church believed that someday Christ would return with a power even greater than that wielded by Moses. Thus for Jesus to say to the Pharisees that the kingdom is already—now—in the midst of them in its most powerful aspect is not quite true to much of the Biblical material.

The third alternative is to distinguish between the kingdom of God on earth and the kingdom of God in heaven. The kingdom of God in heaven is fully obedient to the will of God, which is why we are to pray that God's will may be done on earth as it is done in heaven. If when Jesus answered the Pharisees he was referring to the kingdom of God in heaven, and if there is some validity in my speculation that Einstein's curvature of space provides the clue to the "place" where heaven is, then perhaps Jesus meant quite literally that the kingdom of God or of heaven is "in the midst of" us, although it is invisible. *Heaven may be an entirely different universe right in the midst of us.*

From an exegetical, and also from a scientific, point of view I may be stretching the implications of the ideas of "in the midst of you" and "the curvature of space." But if we are to take the idea of heaven seriously, then we have to attempt to reconcile two difficult facts: "the things that are seen are transient, but the things that are unseen are eternal" (II Corinthians 4:18); and just as angels seem to be physical, and as the resurrection body of Christ seemed to be physical, it would seem to follow that we need a "resurrection universe" *which is invisible and yet allows for bodily existence*. The Bible comes close to saying that this invisible universe is in the midst of us, invisible due to its different spatial curvature.

THE LOCKED ROOMS AND THE SPACE TUNNEL

On at least two occasions after his Resurrection Jesus came and stood in the midst of the disciples when the doors of the room had been shut, and presumably locked, "for fear of the Jews" (John 20:19). On the first occasion Thomas was not with the disciples, but "eight days later, his disciples were again in the house, and Thomas was with them. The doors were shut, but Jesus came and stood among them, and said, 'Peace be with you.' Then he said to Thomas, 'Put your finger here, and see my hands; and put out your hand, and place it in my side; do not be faithless, but believing.' Thomas answered him, 'My Lord and my God!' Jesus said to him, 'Have you believed because you have seen me? Blessed are those who have not seen and yet believe' " (John 20:26–29).

The disciples seemed to have had no explanation of how Jesus could have come and stood in the midst of them while the door was closed. Scholars have sometimes suggested that the resurrection body of Christ was able to go through closed doors, which perhaps it could, but the disciples did not report "seeing" his body somehow move through a closed door. The Gospel of John simply says,

"Jesus came." It strikes one as peculiar that the body of Jesus could move through a door and yet be touched by Thomas, as the Gospel reports in the same sequence. If we can suppose, however, that we live in the "midst" of an invisible spatially curved resurrection universe, then perhaps Jesus "came" through a "space tunnel" into the room where the disciples were gathered with the door locked. The implication would then seem to follow that Jesus did not need a UFO or "space cloud" to take him to heaven, but rather that the Ascension was a special event staged for the benefit of the disciples to let them know that there was something "final" about the way Jesus left on this occasion.

When Jesus appeared to Mary, he said to her, "Do not hold me, for I have not yet ascended to the Father; but go to my brethren and say to them, I am ascending to my Father and your Father, to my God and your God" (John 20:17). Later Jesus invited the disciples to touch him, so that it seems strange that Jesus would have forbidden Mary to "hold" him, although he may have meant, "Do not detain me." But Jesus is reported to have said that he was preparing to ascend to his Father, when in fact the Ascension did not take place for some forty days. On the basis of the resurrection appearances of Jesus one could argue that Jesus actually "moved back and forth" between our world and the resurrection world for the "forty-day" period, appearing to the disciples for short periods of time and then "ascending" or returning to the resurrection world. Jesus was *seen* to ascend on only one occasion, which was his final appearance except for his brief visit to Paul on the Damascus Road. If we can suppose that there is an invisible resurrection universe in the midst of us, then we have a possible explanation of the unusual features of the resurrection appearances of Christ.

There are at least two other occasions reported in the Bible which, while not duplicating the "closed door" resurrection appearances of Christ, may be related to them. On one occasion the apostles were being kept in a guarded prison, and an angel came and set them free. When the officers came for their prisoners, they said they found "the sentries standing at the doors, but when we opened it we found no one inside" (Acts 5:23). The disciples were found teaching in the Temple.

On a second occasion Peter was imprisoned, and "was sleeping between two soldiers, bound with two chains, and sentries before the door were guarding the prison; and behold, an angel of the Lord appeared, and a light shone in the cell; and he struck Peter on the side and woke him, saying, 'Get up quickly.' And the chains fell off his hands" (Acts 12:6, 7). Peter dressed, thinking all the while that he must be dreaming. "When they had passed the first and the second guard, they came to the iron gate leading into the city. It opened to them of its own accord, and they went out and passed on through one street; and immediately the angel left him" (Acts 12:10, 11). Peter was on his own, standing alone in a street in the middle of the night. He finally came to his senses and went his way.

One cannot help wondering how the angel and Peter could get by the sentries undetected, but one also wonders how the angel entered the prison. We read that the iron gate opened to let Peter and the angel out of the prison. Did the angel close the gate when he came in, or did he get in some other way? Did he come in through a space tunnel from the resurrection universe?

Perhaps this is unfounded speculation, but it appears that if we are going to explain much of the Biblical data, the idea of an invisible resurrection universe in the midst of us is an extremely useful idea by which to interpret, or at least make some sense of, much of the Biblical material.

"In My Father's House Are Many Rooms"

There is one aspect of the Biblical view of space which does not directly support our thesis concerning a "resurrection universe" in the midst of us. The Jewish temple provided the "model" by which the Hebrews understood the universe; in fact, the temple provided a microcosmic model of the universe, including heaven and hell. Each part of the temple, the design of which was apparently dictated by an angel, was symbolic of some part of the "house" of God, that is, of God's universe. Thus we read in the Gospel of John that in the words of Jesus, "In my Father's house are many rooms; if it were not so, would I have told you that I go to prepare a place for you? And when I go and prepare a place for you, I will come again and will take you to myself, that where I am you may be also" (John 14:2, 3).

To describe the universe as composed of "rooms" or "compartments" which are spatially separated by "walls" is not quite consistent with my suggestion that two "rooms" or universes occupy the same space. The Bible suggests that we can move from one universe to another, or one room to another, through "doors." The book of Revelation, which is part of the Johannine material, is filled with symbolism related to the Jewish temple. Thus when we read how John received the Apocalypse we discover, "After this I looked, and lo, in heaven an open door! And the first voice, which I had heard speaking to me like a trumpet, said, 'Come up hither, and I will show you what must take place after this.' At once I was in the Spirit, and lo, a throne stood in heaven, with one seated on the throne" (Revelation 4:1–2). When we read in the passages concerning the baptism of Jesus that the Spirit of God descended after the heavens had "opened," we have again an illustration of the way in which the Biblical world view included a many-roomed universe. Heaven was apparently "above," and one entered it by doors. The temple could never provide an adequate model for a universe in which several "universes" coexist one inside the other, for the temple is only three-dimensional, whereas Einstein's universe and related models are more complex.

If one insists on taking the idea of the Jewish temple as a precise model of the universe, one has to assume that space is square, and thus the earth would have "four corners," as would a room in the temple. This is not a useful approach to the problem. But I do not want completely to abandon the idea that the temple may indeed tell us something useful about our universe, and about the relation between our universe, the resurrection world, and hell. These worlds seem to be separated by "walls" of some sort, and spatial curvatures according to modern science form "natural" walls. Jesus told of the fact that our status in the next world, whether in heaven or in hell, depends on our deeds in this life. He spoke of a rich man who refused to feed the poor man Lazarus. Both died, the rich man going to Hades, and Lazarus to the bosom of Abraham. The rich man called to Abraham for help, but help could not be given, among other reasons, because "besides all this, between us and you a great chasm has been fixed, in order that those who would pass from here to you may not be able, and none may cross from there to us" (Luke 16:26). The word *chasm* is used here by Luke, and this is the only occasion on which the word is used in the whole New Testament. The Greek word quite literally means "a yawning";[11] a "yawning," or bending of space so that it is impossible to move from one space to another, suggests that the "rooms" in God's "house" are separated by something like a bending or yawning or curvature of space.

We must keep in mind the extreme hazards of trying to give a factual interpretation of Biblical material which is symbolic in nature. Should one apply this symbolism to modern theories of space, which are by no means universally accepted among scientists and may be radically revised in the future? I do not know. But I do believe that the relation between the Biblical view of space and our modern views of space is extremely *open*. To speak, as Bishop Robinson does, about the primitive Biblical three-decker universe does not begin to explore the delicate aspects of the Biblical view of space. Our understanding of space has changed so radically in the past fifty years that it is difficult for anyone except scientific and mathematical specialists to understand what the modern views of space are.

We should be prepared to tolerate a less than perfect spatial "model" which may have been used by the beings from another world who seem to have helped shape the Biblical view of space. If we allow ourselves to be a little "liberal" in our interpretation of the Biblical cosmology, and if we are also a little "liberal" in our interpretation of our modern cosmologies—that is, if we admit that the situation is extremely open—then I cannot see how the "demythologizers" can be so certain that the Biblical world view and our modern world view do not, and never will, fit together, and that as a consequence it is in Bishop Robinson's opinion "intellectually dishonest" for a Christian even to go on hoping that Jesus really was "lifted up" into space by some sort of UFO—a space cloud—or that there may really be an invisible heaven and hell. Robinson can argue that many of my speculations are "highly improbable," perhaps ridiculous, but we are a long way from the point where we can say that the whole Biblical way of thinking about space is *impossible*—which is what Robinson is in effect saying. It would be a mistake to take everything the Bible says about space literally, but I believe it would also be a mistake to suppose that the Bible tells us nothing true or important concerning space.

CHAPTER VI

FLYING SAUCERS AND THE FUTURE

Speaking about "flying saucers and the future" may immediately bring to mind the question of whether or not UFOs carrying beings from another world might someday land in force on earth. This is in fact what the Bible predicts, but not in the sense which modern UFO writers suggest. It may be that some or many of our modern UFOs carry beings from another planet, and perhaps someday they will land, and we can exchange scientific information with them, or trade animals with them; we might start an "interplanetary zoo." There are all kinds of possibilities in this realm, but the possibility also exists in the Biblical realm, in terms of the day of judgment and the second coming of Christ.

When Jesus was taken up into heaven in a "space cloud," two men "in white robes" said to the disciples, "This Jesus, who was taken up from you into heaven, will come in the same way as you saw him go into heaven" (Acts 1:11). The New Testament indicates that in the future Jesus will return to earth in triumph, glory, and judgment. At this time of judgment the "dead" will be raised, and will be carried to heaven. It is extremely hazardous, even from the scientific point of view, to try to "predict" the future, and yet empirical philosophy is quite convinced that the best type of scientific verification—or falsification—is based on prediction and fulfillment. Thus a good scientist may predict an eclipse—and if he is a good scientist, the eclipse will occur as predicted. The Bible predicts many things, but in particular it predicts (or prophesies) that Christ will return in the future and that all men will be raised from the dead, some to salvation and some to damnation. The concept of flying saucers helps clarify what for some people may seem like strange doctrines. In the Apostles' Creed Christians state that they believe that Christ ascended into heaven, and "from thence he shall come to judge the quick and the dead. I believe in . . . the resurrection of the body; and the life everlasting." Thus when we speak of "flying saucers and the future," we have in mind not so much interplanetary cultural and scientific exchange as the eternal future of every person on the face of the earth. It is because of the *eternal* implications of flying saucers that the idea of flying saucers is so important. If flying saucers contain beings from another planet who may soon contact us, this is also important. But if flying saucers contain beings from the resurrection world about which the Bible

192

speaks, and *if the Biblical religion provides the clue to eternal existence,* then flying saucers gain eternal significance. Eternity may be more important to some people than interplanetary cultural exchanges. In this chapter we shall examine two extremely difficult Biblical concepts, both of which are eschatological and both of which are related to UFOs: flying saucers and the second coming of Christ, and flying saucers and the resurrection of the body.

FLYING SAUCERS AND THE SECOND COMING OF CHRIST

There have been two major pitfalls throughout the history of the Church in regard to the doctrine of the second coming of Christ: There have been those who have sought to "predict" the date of the second coming, and there have been those who have sought to dismiss the doctrine entirely.

At the Ascension the apostles were told by two beings from another world that Christ would someday return in the same manner as he ascended into heaven. Bishop Robinson, in dismissing the Ascension of Christ, by consequence must dismiss the doctrine of the second coming. The disciples, just before the Ascension, asked Jesus "Lord, will you at this time restore the kingdom to Israel?" (Acts 1:6). The answer Jesus gave has unfortunately been ignored by a segment of the Church. Jesus said, "It is not for you to know times or seasons which the Father has fixed by his own authority" (Acts 1:7). If Jesus would not reveal the date of his second coming to his disciples, we can hardly expect him to reveal the date to someone in the middle of the twentieth century. It is possible that Jesus himself did not know the "date" of his apocalyptic coming, for on one occasion he said, "But of that day and hour no one knows, not even the angels of heaven, nor the Son, but the Father only" (Matthew 24:36). The only clear advice in the Bible is shown in the parable concerning the wise and foolish maidens waiting for the coming of the bridegroom (Christ). Jesus concluded, "Watch therefore, for you know neither the day nor the hour" (Matthew 25:13).

Isaac Newton, who is admired as one of the greatest scientists of all time, was also an excellent, though hetero-dox, theologian. His favorite Biblical book was the Revelation to John, a book which had often been used by theologians as the basis on which to "predict" the second coming of Christ, together with other historical events. But Newton made no predictions concerning the second coming of Christ, although he was firmly convinced that the second coming would someday occur. Newton said in reference to the Apocalypse:

> The folly of interpreters hath been, to foretell times and things by this prophecy, as if God designed to make them prophets. By this rashness they have not only exposed themselves, but brought the prophecy also into contempt. The design of God was much otherwise. He gave this, and the prophecies of the Old Testament, not to gratify men's curiosities by enabling them to foreknow things; but that, after they were fulfilled, they might be interpreted by the event, and his own Providence, not the interpreters, be then manifested thereby to the world.[1]

Thus, while I think that flying saucers provide an excellent means of entering into the Biblical thinking concerning the second coming, we are by no means in any better position to predict any dates. Nearly two thousand years have elapsed since the "first coming," and there may be two thousand or two hundred thousand years between now and the second coming.

But while I do not believe that we should predict dates, I also do not believe that we should give up the idea of the second coming. The trend in theology since the nineteenth century has been to reject the idea of the second coming of Christ. This rejection was summarized and crystallized in Albert Schweitzer's work *The Quest of the Historical Jesus.*[2] The early Church apparently expected that Christ would return in triumph and glory within a few years— perhaps within the lifetime of most of the new converts. This expectation of an early return, of "the eschaton," helped missionary fervor, but as the coming was "delayed," questions arose about the doctrine. Schweitzer and others have argued that since the second coming has been delayed for nearly two thousand years, it appears that Jesus, or the early Church, or both, were deluded concerning this doctrine. It is clear that in the Bible the "time" element was never settled. Schweitzer has argued in effect that since the second coming has not occurred yet, it will never occur. As time goes on, this argument becomes more convincing. But if Christ should return, that would end the argument.

What does the New Testament indicate concerning the manner of the second coming of Christ? The manner is usually expressed in "apocalyptic" language, which is quite different from narrative. Many Christian scholars have given apocalyptic messages historical interpretation, and the combination of the idea of "flying saucers" and certain of the apocalyptic sayings attributed to Jesus offers a possible historical explanation or prediction of the second coming.

Here is one passage of Scripture attributed to Jesus which apparently relates to his second coming. "Immediately after the tribulation of those days the sun will be darkened, and the moon will not give its light, and the stars will fall from heaven, and the powers of the heavens will be shaken; then will appear the sign of the Son of man in heaven, and then all the tribes of the earth will mourn, and they will see the Son of man coming on the clouds of heaven with power and great glory; and he will send out his angels with a loud trumpet call, and they will gather his elect from the four winds, from one end of heaven to the other" (Matthew 24:29–31). Some interpreters suppose that the sun, the moon, and the stars are symbolic of various earthly rulers and kingdoms and thus tend to give the passage a totally historical interpretation without any understanding of a disturbance in nature; that is, they do not expect the celestial stars to fall, but rather the kings and presidents on earth to be the "falling stars," who will be replaced by the Son of Man.

On the other hand, there do appear to be "heavenly" aspects to this passage. There is the problem of what is signified by "the sign of the Son of man in heaven," and also the fact that all the tribes on earth "will see the Son of man coming on the clouds of heaven with power and great glory." The idea of the coming of the Son "with the clouds of heaven" has its origin in a vision of the Prophet Daniel (Daniel 7:13), the only occasion on which the phrase *clouds of heaven* is used in the Old Testament. It seems reasonable to conjecture that there is some connection between the "pillar of cloud" or the bright cloud of

God's glory which led Israel through the Red Sea and the idea of "clouds of heaven." The "pillar of cloud" presumably originated in heaven. In the Old Testament there is nothing that parallels the New Testament understanding of heaven, although the Old Testament people seem to have believed in life after death. It is only with Christ that the idea of heaven really comes into its own, for he claims to have originated in heaven—as he said, "For I have come down from heaven" (John 6:38). When Daniel uses the phrase *clouds of heaven,* he does not make any reference to the glory of God, but in this passage in Matthew the heavenly clouds seem to supply the "power and great glory," which is quite consistent with the Mosaic tradition and with the bright cloud of the Transfiguration. At the Ascension it was reported that Jesus was "lifted up" and taken away in a cloud, and the two men standing by in "white robes" reported that Jesus "will come in the same way as you saw him go into heaven" (Acts 1:11). If the Ascension is a historical event, and if the prophecies concerning the second coming are to be interpreted in a way which is consistent with the Ascension passage, it is permissible to say that Jesus will return to judge the earth in a flying-saucer-like UFO, his space cloud, his heavenly cloud.

The other thing to notice about this whole sequence in Matthew is that Jesus does not intend to return alone. Whereas throughout the whole New Testament the power of God is underplayed, the gospel is hidden in the lump, at the day of judgment, and of the second coming, the power which was seen in the UFO at the Red Sea will once again be seen, this time in connection with Christ. Previously the power of Christ was hidden, but in the future his lordship will be made manifest over the whole earth, he will return in some sort of UFO with great power and glory (brightness), "and he will send out his angels with a loud trumpet call." At the second coming Christ will not return alone, but rather will have a whole army of angels.

Matthew on several occasions connects judgment and the second coming with angels. "Just as the weeds are gathered and burned with fire, so will it be at the close of the age. The Son of man will send his angels, and they will gather out of his kingdom all causes of sin and all evildoers, and throw them into the furnace of fire; there men will weep and gnash their teeth. Then the righteous will shine like the sun in the kingdom of their Father. He who has ears, let him hear" (Matthew 13:40–43). Both Mark and Luke bear witness in parallel passages to this basic apocalyptic perspective. One suspects that a whole "fleet" of UFOs would be required to bring this "army" of angels. "For the Son of man is to come with his angels in the glory of his Father, and then he will repay every man for what he has done" (Matthew 16:27), and when he has returned with these angels, Christ "will sit on his glorious throne" (Matthew 25:31). The Gospel of John indicates that these angels come through an "opening" in the heavens (John 1:51). Christ compares his coming to the flood which came during the days of Noah (Matthew 24:37–39), and also to the raining of fire and brimstone on Sodom (Luke 17:28–30). As the floods of water and fire came suddenly upon the earth, so will the flood of angels with their leader, the Son of man. "For as the lightning flashes and lights up the sky from one side to the other, so will the Son of man be in his day" (Luke 17:24).

Modern flying saucers have recorded speeds estimated on radar in excess of 18,000 miles per hour. Whether or not something like flying saucers will execute the second coming of Christ together with an army of beings from another world I do not know, but at the present time I do not see any way this can be ruled out. Apocalyptic language is "cloudy," and when Christians do not know the exact or proper interpretation of an obscure passage, they must have the courage to say that they do not know the answer. But the fact is that if flying saucers do exist, then we would have what empirical philosophers such as Wittgenstein have suggested the Christian faith does not have; that is, an empirical basis for the verification (or falsification) of Christian religious statements. Some Christian scholars have suggested that life after death—life in the resurrection world—might constitute a basis for empirical verification of Christianity. But philosophers generally have objected to the idea of placing verification in an invisible realm. Flying saucers, and the possibility of the second coming of Christ, open up the possibility that the Christian faith could be verified or falsified in this world. This would mean that religious statements are open to verification, and are either true or false, and not *meaningless* as some philosophers have suggested.

We have not "proved" that the Christian religion is true, although we are trying to discover evidence which will give the faith a greater degree of probability; but obviously many areas of doubt remain. Ritchie Calder, in his book *Science in Our Lives,* suggested that "Science has been defined as 'Proof without Certainty' and Faith as 'Certainty without Proof.' " [3] Unfortunately, Christians sometimes try to claim more "certainty" than they have a right to, and they may attempt to shame their fellow Christians who have doubts. Christ did want men to be certain about him, but one cannot force oneself to believe by pulling up on his own bootstraps of faith. Faith comes through hearing and seeing, as the disciples saw and heard Christ. You do not have to see and touch Christ to believe; you can trust the eyewitness reports. Seeing is not necessarily believing. When Christ appeared after his Resurrection to his disciples, "some doubted" (Matthew 28:17). When we witness an event which is contrary to all other human experience, we may discount it. The Christian life is not one of total certainty—as Paul maintained, we walk by faith, not by sight, "for now we see in a mirror dimly" (I Corinthians 13:12). When a person confesses belief in Christ, God is at work (Matthew 16:17); no one can accept Christ on the basis of simply seeing Christ perform miracles; no one comes to Christ, according to Jesus, "unless the Father who sent me draws him" (John 6:44).

The whole problem of belief, doubt, certainty, and proof is very complicated in the light of the Biblical material, and the problems focus around how one knows the truth. Even people who see the truth will not recognize it if they are not prepared inwardly—psychologically—to accept the truth when they see it. A Christian is a person who has decided prayerfully, intellectually, and scientifically that all the inward and outward evidence has led him to base his life on the assumption (correct or incorrect) that Jesus is the Son of God, that he died for the sins of men, that he rose from the dead, and that one day he will return to raise all men from the dead. This is an "operational definition" of a Christian. Physical evidence, or scientific evidence, of the resurrection is not enough to make a person a Christian. A person also needs the resurrected Christ "living within him." A man needs both physical and spiritual evidence. Psychology and medicine are now beginning to see that the physical and mental are intimately linked. Man needs an internal and external witness to the resurrection, and it would seem to be a duty of the Church to make the Biblical witness to the physical resurrection as probable (scientifically and Biblically) as possible. While I would not say, using Calder's terms, that we can have "proof of the resurrection without certainty," nevertheless I would say that there are degrees of evidence which make the physical resurrection either more or less probable. If Jesus really is the Christ, the evidence will eventually show this to be the case.

The suggestion that science is proof without certainty and faith is certainty without proof may arise from the Biblical distinction between the sheep and the goats, or between light and darkness. But there are shades of light and darkness: some sheep are more faithful than others; occasionally there is the lost sheep. In one parable Jesus speaks of a sower who went out to sow: some seeds were devoured by the birds; some fell on rocky ground, sprouted, but were quickly scorched by the sun; other seed fell among thorns and was choked out by them; but still other seed fell in good soil bringing forth grain, "yielding thirtyfold and sixtyfold and a hundredfold" (Mark 4:8). The concept of yield may point to "works" rather than "faith," but faith and faithfulness are directly proportional according to Biblical thinking. Thus it seems that there is something like a matter of "degree" in the concept of faith, just as truth in science is a matter of degree or probability. A Christian might be a person who is convinced that there is a 60 per cent chance that Jesus is the Christ—in both a conscious and subconscious sense—and he might accordingly yield twentyfold. It is conceivable that a person might think there is less than 1 per cent chance that Jesus is the Christ, and he still might decide that he wanted to live out his life as a Christian, although this seems unlikely. This is a rather "mechanical" analysis of a parable which is expressed in organic terms of life. But the breach between science and faith does not seem to be the difference in the way each interprets the nature of proof and certainty.

Three decades ago Enrico Fermi postulated that a very peculiar "something" or form of energy was missing from an atomic equation. Fermi knew the *quantity* of energy which was missing, but he concluded that this energy had neither a positive nor a negative charge, it had no mass, and because of these properties he named it the "neutrino." Fermi's neutrino caused a considerable scandal in the field of science because no one could capture it—it had very elusive properties. Some scientists were certain that the whole idea was a fraud, that such an energy particle just did not exist. Some scientists thought that it might even be "intellectually dishonest" to continue to discuss the neutrino and its role in atomic physics. But other men were convinced that the neutrino was "there" and that eventually it could be captured. Stubborn scientists who "believed in the neutrino" even though no one had ever seen it or seen any experimental sign of it tried experiments with scintillation counters for several years until finally they succeeded in "capturing" the neutrino, in showing that the neutrino existed.[4] What can be said about the mental state of those scientists who persisted in looking for the neutrino? St. Anselm would have said that these were men of faith who were seeking understanding—*fides quarens intellectum.* A Christian can have "faith" that the second coming of Christ will occur; interpreting the second coming in relation to flying saucers may be one way— or perhaps the way—in which the second coming may be understood. The man of science and the man of faith are not in very different positions in respect to their methods, although their subject matter is, of course, different. Both scientists and theologians very often have to repent— they make mistakes—but occasionally they stumble onto the truth, one brick at a time.

FLYING SAUCERS AND THE RESURRECTION OF THE BODY

The New Testament maintains that all men shall some- day be raised from the dead in a new body—a resurrection body. It is this doctrine above all others which has led critics to say that the Christian faith offers pie in the sky bye and bye. More precisely, however, all will be raised; not everyone gets to eat pie. Those who do not obey the gospel of Christ "shall suffer the punishment of eternal destruction and exclusion from the presence of the Lord" (II Thessalonians 1:9). The resurrection of all men is usually, although not always, closely linked with the sec- ond coming of Christ; furthermore, the resurrection world is the world of angels. We might expect that there would be some link between the idea of flying saucers and the Biblical concept of the resurrection. We shall examine briefly only two basic questions: (1) When will the resur- rection take place, and (2) How will it take place?

The resurrection will take place either immediately after a person dies, or at the second coming of Christ, or perhaps a combination or variation of both times.

While Jesus was dying on the cross, one of the two thieves who was crucified at the same time apparently accepted Christ and his kingly power. Jesus said to him, "today you will be with me in Paradise" (Luke 23:43). The Apostle Paul believed that if he died he would join Christ immediately. He says, "I am hard pressed between the two. My desire is to depart and be with Christ, for that is far better. But to remain in the flesh is more necessary on your account" (Philippians 1:23, 24). He can also say that Christians "long to put on our heavenly dwelling" (II Corinthians 5:2), that is, their heavenly body. We have also seen in the Gospels that Jesus thought Abraham witnessed his coming. Moses and Elijah apparently met with Christ, Peter, James, and John at the Mount of Transfiguration. There are certainly enough passages in the Bible which indicate little if any delay between this life and the next so that it can be argued that life after death is immediate. There were only three days between the death and the Resurrection of Christ, whether or not this has any relevance here.

On the other hand, Jesus said that "every one who sees the Son and believes in him should have eternal life; and I will raise him up at the last day" (John 6:40). The "last day" is the Judgment Day, the day of Christ's second coming. In one of his letters Paul talks about those Christians who have "fallen asleep"—that is, died—before the coming of Christ. Paul explains that in the day of judgment those who have "fallen asleep" will be raised and taken to the Lord first, and they will be followed by those who are still alive on earth (I Thessalonians 4:13–18). We shall discuss this passage in detail when we examine the "how" of the resurrection. But for the moment we can conclude that there is considerable Biblical evidence that the resurrection will not take place until the second coming of Christ.

The third alternative is to believe in *two resurrections*. The book of Revelation speaks about a special group of Christians, apparently martyrs, who were raised to life again, and they "reigned with Christ a thousand years. The rest of the dead did not come to life again until the thousand years were ended. This is the first resurrection" (Revelation 20:4, 5). It could be argued that God raises some of the special saints and prophets either immediately or ahead of everyone else. Elijah was taken up into heaven immediately, and Moses and Abraham seem to be alive. Perhaps the apostles have also shared in an early resurrection; Paul may have known that this applied to him (Philippians 1:23, 24).

The problem of the "when" of the resurrection has caused considerable controversy in the Church for some time. Unfortunately, the concept of flying saucers does not clarify the passages which deal with the "when" of the resurrection, any more than UFOs clarify the passages dealing with the "when" of the second coming of Christ.

But if UFOs do not solve the problem of the "when" of the resurrection, they do shed some light on a possible explanation of the "how" of the resurrection. Let us examine Paul's description of the second coming and the day of resurrection in I Thessalonians: "For the Lord himself will descend from heaven with a cry of command, with the archangel's call, and with the sound of the trumpet of God.

And the dead in Christ will rise first; then we who are alive, who are left, shall be caught up together with them in the clouds to meet the Lord in the air; and so we shall always be with the Lord" (I Thessalonians 4:16, 17). The second coming of Christ heralds the day of resurrection. Christ expected to return from heaven "in the clouds" with angels and with great power. Paul also adds that both those "asleep" and those "alive" shall be "caught up" "in the clouds to meet the Lord in the air." If we substitute "UFOs" or "flying saucers" for clouds, the passage is consistent with scientific possibility.

There is one other occasion on which Paul speaks of being "caught up," which in the Greek suggests that one is taken up by force, and this is how Paul describes his experience in II Corinthians. He speaks about his own "revelations," although to avoid boasting he speaks as if he were talking about another man. He says, "I know a man in Christ who fourteen years ago was caught up to the third heaven—whether in the body or out of the body I do not know, God knows. And I know that this man was caught up into Paradise—whether in the body or out of the body I do not know, God knows—and he heard things that cannot be told" (II Corinthians 12:2-4). There is a real tension in the mind of Paul on this occasion as to whether he was "caught up" in his own body or not. Since Paul did not know, we can hardly know, but he himself could not rule out the possibility that he was somehow "caught up," forcefully taken to "Paradise" in his own earthly body where he saw and heard unspeakable things. Either Paul was lost for words, or else he did not understand the heavenly language. In keeping with our earlier discussion on the "degrees of faith" and the degrees of verification to which a Christian may be subjected, it is fair to say that if Paul endured the experience of being taken away to Paradise in some sort of UFO, a "heavenly cloud," then we can well understand his firm conviction concerning the Lordship of Christ, and the future resurrected life in Paradise. In this passage in II Corinthians Paul does not mention any sort of UFO as being responsible for the fact that he was "caught up," but it would certainly have been consistent with his Damascus Road experience, and his discussion in I Thessalonians of the experience of being "caught up" in the "clouds" at the second coming of Christ.

Returning to I Thessalonians, we have seen that those who have been raised from the dead will be forcefully taken "in the clouds to meet the Lord in the air." If we interpret the word *cloud* in a straightforward sense, we of course have difficulty scientifically seeing what Paul could mean. But if we interpret the passage in the light of modern UFOs, the situation changes.

This passage in I Thessalonians also brings to mind the fact that angels, apparently in charge of a fleet of "clouds," will help execute the day of judgment and resurrection. In telling the story of the rich man and Lazarus, Jesus said, "The poor man died and was carried by the angels to Abraham's bosom" (Luke 16:22). Here again is an indication that angels have something to do with the transportation of the resurrected person to his eternal abiding place.

Interpreting the concept of the resurrection in light of flying saucers underlines more than ever the fact that man's future life in heaven will be spent in a body of some kind. What will this body be like? Paul speaks much about the resurrection body, which he once described as a "spiritual body" (I Corinthians 15:44), but we have seen that he simply means that this is a body which will be appropriate for man's heavenly existence. Paul uses the word *spiritual* here because it is the opposite of *physical*, and it fits the pattern of opposites in this whole passage. He says, "What is sown is perishable, what is raised is imperishable. It is sown in dishonor, it is raised in glory. It is sown in weakness, it is raised in power. It is sown a physical body, it is raised a spiritual body. If there is a physical body, there is also a spiritual body" (I Corinthians 15:42–44). Realizing that the term *spiritual body* is almost self-contradictory—spiritual and body—Paul adds an extra sentence to apologize for putting these opposites together. "If there is a physical body, there is also a spiritual body."

In II Corinthians Paul speaks of man's resurrection body as a "heavenly dwelling," which is equivalent to his idea of a spiritual body. He says, "For we know that if the earthly tent we live in is destroyed, we have a building from God, a house not made with hands, eternal in the heavens. Here indeed we groan, and long to put on our heavenly dwelling, so that . . . what is mortal may be swallowed up by life" (II Corinthians 5:1–4). The term *heavenly body* would be the best way to describe our resurrection body, for the term *spiritual body* can be somewhat misleading, as Paul seems to have realized. If the resurrection body of Christ is the prototype of the resurrection body of all Christians, then it seems clear that man's "heavenly dwelling" or "spiritual body" can be concrete enough so that Thomas could touch it.

One can certainly argue, however, that the resurrection body of Christ was no ordinary body, and certainly neither

the Bible as a whole, nor the Apostle Paul, maintains that
the resurrection body is identical in form or content with
man's earthly body. While Thomas did touch Christ, Christ
appeared after the doors were shut—whether Christ came
through a "space tunnel" or whether his resurrection body
could move through closed doors we do not know. Jesus
appeared to, and walked with, two disciples on the Em-
maus Road, but somehow the disciples did not recognize
Jesus: "But their eyes were kept from recognizing him"
(Luke 24:16). Luke lays the fault on the eyes of the disciples rather than on the body or appearance of Jesus.
Their eyes were "opened" when Christ broke bread before
them, and after they recognized him, he "vanished" (Luke
24:31).

Christians have long argued concerning the relation
between the old and the new body. Some have supposed
that every "atom" which was in a person's body when he
died would somehow become reunited to form the resurrection body. But many informed Christians have realized
that when a person dies his body decays and may become
fertilizer for plants, which in turn can produce fruit for
another man to eat. What about the atom which belonged
to the body of two or more men (separated in time)? This
sort of argument took place before the atom was smashed
and before demythologizing, so this argument seems peculiar. Part of the difficulty may lie in the fact that men have
used the Resurrection of Christ as a precise model by
which to understand our own resurrection, which may not
be the best policy. Luke records that when the women
came to the tomb on the first day of the week, they found
the stone rolled away, "but when they went in they did
not find the body" (Luke 24:3), that is, the dead body

of Christ. They found an empty tomb, except that two men in "dazzling apparel" were present to explain that Christ had risen. This sequence suggests an almost one-to-one relation or continuity between the earthly body of Christ and his resurrection body, but are we justified in trying to find in Christ's Resurrection a precise model for our own resurrection? Christ's Resurrection did for the apostles what the experience of being "caught up" to Paradise did for Paul: it gave them a firm impression of the message they were to preach and a more complete perspective of God's plan for mankind.

Perhaps the best way to understand the relation between our earthly and heavenly body is to use, with the Apostle Paul, the analogy of the seed. Paul has been stressing how important it is to believe in the resurrection. He says, "But some one will ask, 'How are the dead raised? With what kind of body do they come?' You foolish man! What you sow does not come to life unless it dies. And what you sow is not the body which is to be, but a bare kernel, perhaps of wheat or of some other grain. But God gives it a body as he has chosen, and to each kind of seed its own body. For not all flesh is alike, but there is one kind for men, another for animals, another for birds, and another for fish. There are celestial bodies and there are terrestrial bodies; but the glory of the celestial is one, and the glory of the terrestrial is another. . . . So is it with the resurrection of the dead. What is sown is perishable, what is raised is imperishable" (I Corinthians 15:35–40, 42).

There are two warrantable conclusions which can be drawn from this passage concerning the relation between the earthly body and the resurrection body. The resurrection body has a higher degree of "glory," or brightness (as the clothing of angels seems to be bright), than man's earthly body. It is more desirable, as it is more desirable to have the body of a man than of a fish (presumably). Notice that if our earthly body is the "seed" for our resurrection body, then there is apparently some continuity between our world and the resurrection world. Human "seeds," the male sperm and the female egg in this life, carry chromosomes which determine the physical characteristics which will be part of the new body which grows from the union of the sperm and egg. How we might find an analogy in our own body and in the resurrection body to parallel the idea of genes and chromosomes is difficult. Perhaps this is what the Bible means by the idea of the human "soul"; if Paul is correct in saying that there will be some continuity between our earthly body and our heavenly body, then perhaps there is some kind of "energy precipitate" which, like a tape recording or like the DNA molecule, can be carried through time and space and then be "played back" when the desired moment and place are found. There is a new type of instant coffee which is made by percolating the coffee in the manufacturing plant, freezing the "cup" of coffee, and evaporating the frozen liquid until crystals are formed, which are then shipped to market for distribution. When coffee is desired, hot water is added to the "precipitated" or "freeze-dried" particles of coffee. Perhaps when the human body dies, there is some human "energy precipitate" which can later transfer the real stuff of human personality—the coffee—to a new body. Absurd speculation perhaps, but analogy seems to be the only route by which the resurrection can be understood from the human side. In his well-known book *Varieties of Religious Experience,* William James has recorded experiences of persons feeling the presence of an unseen force.[5] Others have reported being by the bedside to witness the death of an individual, and supposedly seeing a glowing light energy leave the dead body. Whether or not this light energy points to an "energy precipitate" or to what Paul calls the "seed" which will sometime be transformed into the resurrection body, only time will tell.

Where Do We Go from Here?

First of all, I believe that we must be willing to accept a kind of principle of uncertainty in our search for truth. This is not only a scientific principle, but it appears to have been the basis of man's response to God, since men from Abraham to the Apostle Paul have walked by faith, not by sure knowledge. We have to be willing to live in a state of tension, a state of expectation that in time the truth will more completely unfold. I have frequently been asked, "Do you yourself believe that the parting of the Red Sea was caused by some sort of UFO?" My answer is "Yes, about 80 per cent." I say this because I believe that I must leave room for doubt, so that I will be open to new evidence when it comes in.

My strongest belief is that there is room for much more research within the field I have explored in this book. Not only is there a need for an exhaustive study of the nature and function of the various Biblical reports of UFOs and of the reports concerning the appearance of angels, but there is a need to study related subjects such as the glory of God and the throne of God, in both the Old and the New Testaments. We have left untouched the whole problem of evil, including "the devil and his angels" (Matthew 25:41), although it is worth mentioning that by far the majority of Biblical references to angels are to "good" angels.

There is also a need for the theological community to try to maintain better contact with what is happening in the physical sciences. In an age of both theological and scientific specialization this is extremely difficult. An Old Testament archaeologist may not know much more about existential theology than a biochemist knows about geology, and none of these people may know much about cosmological speculation concerning the expanding universe, or experimental confirmation of certain aspects of the theory of relativity. Since new discoveries are constantly being made in each field, it is difficult enough to keep up in a single field without trying to keep up in several fields and build bridges between them. But I believe that many of our current theological problems have arisen because we have not been willing to build the necessary bridges between science and theology. This cannot be a one-man effort. It must become a special field in itself. The bridge between theology and the social sciences has been quite well established and has become a specialized field. But this specialized field has in fact been largely responsible for the death of God theology, which is overwhelmingly oriented toward the psychological sciences. If equal effort had been placed in the attempt to keep up with the physical sciences, we might well have avoided many of the theological problems which now surround us.

I am most anxious to underline that I consider most of

the hypotheses in this book to be quite tentative. I do not doubt that in time my perspective will seem very limited. But it is my hope that I have seen enough to encourage others to take a closer look at the same territory, and to make their reports.

NOTES

CHAPTER I

1. I do not mean to suggest that I am the first writer to consider the possible relation between flying saucers and the Bible. Frank Edwards, in his book *Flying Saucers—Serious Business* (New York, Lyle Stuart, 1966), makes reference to a possible relation between UFOs and the Bible, and mentions a book by Morris Jessup entitled *The UFO and the Bible* (pp. 16 ff. in Edwards's book). Although I have not been able to obtain a copy of the book by Jessup, it is clear that others have thought about the subject. But it is also clear that the relation between the Bible and flying saucers is not being discussed by the professional theological community, as I believe it should be.

2. For a brief discussion of some of the issues involved in the "death of God" theology, see *Time* magazine's cover story, "Is God Dead?" April 8, 1966, pp. 82–87. In this book we shall refer mainly to the work of Thomas J. J. Altizer of Emory University, one of the leaders of the death of God theology.

3. Marshall McLuhan, *Understanding Media: The Extensions of Man* (New York, McGraw, 1964).

4. John A. T. Robinson, *Honest to God* (London, SCM, 1963).

5. *Ibid.*, p. 11.

6. *Ibid.*, p. 13.

7. *Ibid.*, pp. 13–14.

8. *Ibid.*, p. 35.

9. Rudolf Bultmann, *Jesus Christ and Mythology* (New York, Scribner, 1958), pp. 36–37.

10. Robinson, *op. cit.*, p. 33.

11. For an examination of the path by which Altizer arrived at some of his conclusions, see Thomas J. J. Altizer, *Mircea Eliade and the Dialectic of the Sacred* (Philadelphia, Westminster, 1963).

12. James A. Pike, *A Time for Christian Candor* (New York, Harper, 1964).

13. Bultmann, *op. cit.*, p. 36.

14. Robinson, *op. cit.*, p. 28.

15. Sigmar von Fersen, in the *Dictionary of Philosophy*, ed. Dagobert D. Runes (Ames, Iowa, Littlefield, Adams, 1955), p. 102.

16. Bultmann, *op. cit.*, p. 36.

17. *Ibid.*, p. 38.

18. Michael Polanyi, *Personal Knowledge: Towards a Post-Critical Philosophy* (New York, Harper, 1958, rev. ed. 1962), pp. 276–277.

CHAPTER II

1. See *The Works of Aristotle Translated into English*, ed. W. D. Ross, 12 vols. (Oxford, Clarendon, 1928–1952), *Physica*, trans. and ed. R. P. Hardie and R. K. Gaye, 1930. See Aristotle's discussion of the "now" point in time, *Physica*, 219 b12, 219 b16–17, etc. See also *Plato's Cosmology: The 'Timaeus' of Plato Translated with a Running Commentary* by F. M. Cornford (London, Kegan Paul, Trench, Trubner, 1937). On the soul as a self-moving unit point, see *Timaeus*, 44D, 47C, etc.

2. See St. Thomas Aquinas, *The Summa Theologica of St. Thomas Aquinas*, trans. the Fathers of English Dominican Province (London, Washbourne, 1911–1921), "Treatise on Angels," especially Q. 50, pp. 287 ff.

3. Jacob Bronowski, *The Common Sense of Science* (New York, Vintage, N.D.), p. 100.

4. Report by Walter Sullivan, *New York Times News Service*,

recorded in the Rochester, New York, *Democrat and Chronicle*, Section A, page 1, August 14, 1966.

5. Report by Henry Machirella, New York *Daily News*, October 22, 1966, p. 2C.

6. I wrote to the Department of the Air Force, Project Blue Book, and received in return what seemed to be an undated leaflet entitled "Project Blue Book," and the enclosed letter described this as "The current report on Project Blue Book." I am not certain when the report was written. I received the report in early 1966, and the only date on the report was "Jan 65." The quoted statement is found on page 4 of the report I received.

7. *Ibid.*, p. 7.

8. See Donald E. Keyhoe, *The Flying Saucer Conspiracy* (New York, Holt, 1955).

9. Edwards, *Flying Saucers—Serious Business*, p. 14.

10. Keyhoe, *op. cit.*, Chapter 17, "Obreth and the G-Field," pp. 247–262. Also Edwards, *op. cit.*, pp. 193 ff.

11. Associated Press, Erie, Pa.; reported in the Rochester, New York, *Times-Union*, Wednesday, August 3, 1966, p. 10D.

12. *Time*, April 1, 1966, p. 15.

13. *Time*, April 8, 1966, p. 70.

14. J. Allen Hynek, "Are Flying Saucers Real?" *Saturday Evening Post*, December 17, 1966, pp. 17–21.

15. *Time*, April 8, 1966, p. 82.

16. Mircea Eliade, *The Sacred and the Profane: The Nature of Religion*, trans. from the French by Willard R. Trask (New York, Harcourt, 1959).

17. Carl G. Jung, *Flying Saucers: A Modern Myth of Things Seen in the Skies*, trans. R. F. C. Hull (New York, Harcourt, 1959). *Time* is at least consistent in its approach to flying saucers. The August 4, 1967, issue of *Time* includes the essay, "A Fresh Look at Flying Saucers," pp. 32–33, in which the editors take a less skeptical view of saucers, but nevertheless refer to the mythological view of saucers put forward in Jung's book, saying, "One persuasive theory about saucers is that they are real only in the mind."

18. *Fate: True Stories of the Strange and the Unknown*, May, 1966. The articles referred to begin on pp. 84, 53, and 32 respectively.

19. Altizer, *Mircea Eliade and the Dialectic of the Sacred*, p. 13.

20. *Ibid.*, p. 151.

21. Report by Rose Sold, Rochester, New York, *Times-Union*, November 2, 1966, p. 4B.

22. Associated Press, reported in the Rochester, New York, *Times-Union*, November 10, 1966, p. 20B.

23. Robinson, *Honest to God*, p. 15.

Chapter III

1. Robinson, *Honest to God*, p. 33.

2. Jacques Vallee, *Anatomy of a Phenomenon: Unidentified Objects in Space; A Scientific Appraisal* (Chicago, Henry Regnery, 1965), p. 104.

3. G. A. Barrois, in *The Interpreter's Dictionary of the Bible*, ed. George A. Buttrick *et al.* (Nashville, Tennessee, Abingdon, 4 vols., 1962), Vol. III, p. 816.

4. Martin Noth, *Exodus: A Commentary*, trans. J. S. Bowden (Philadelphia, Westminster, 1962), p. 110.

5. This quotation is from the Exegesis of the Book of Exodus by J. Coert Rylaarsdam in *The Interpreter's Bible: The Holy Scriptures in the King James and Revised Standard Versions with General Articles and Introduction, Exegesis, Exposition for Each Book of the Bible*, ed. George A. Buttrick *et al.* (Nashville, Tennessee, Abingdon, 12 vols., 1952), Vol. I, p. 938.

6. Noth, *op. cit.*, p. 116.

7. Associated Press, Wanaque, N.J., reported in *Utica* (N.Y.) *Daily Press*, October 12, 1966, p. 3.

8. Edwards, *Flying Saucers—Serious Business*, reports two separate instances, in one case saying that "a circular patch of tiny waves" moved under the saucer in the water beneath as the saucer moved above (p. 304).

9. Noth, *op. cit.*, p. 115.

10. *Ibid.*, p. 116. The "J" tradition to which Noth refers is one of the three literary strands, known as J, E, and P, that scholars believe were edited to form the book of Exodus.

11. Edwards, *op. cit.*, p. 306.

12. *Ibid.*, p. 303, photo, p. 218.

13. Noth, *op. cit.*, p. 109.

14. A. H. McNeile, *The Book of Exodus* (London, Methuen, N.D.), p. 82.

15. Keyhoe, *The Flying Saucer Conspiracy*, pp. 225–246.

16. Vallee, *op. cit.*, p. 136.

17. Noth, *op. cit.*, p. 109.

18. Coral and Jim Lorenzen, *Flying Saucer Occupants* (A Signet Book: New York, New American Library, 1967), pp. 42–86.

CHAPTER IV

1. C. K. Barrett, *The Holy Spirit and the Gospel Tradition* (New York, Macmillan, 1947), pp. 35–39.
2. Walter Bauer, *A Greek-English Lexicon of the New Testament and Other Early Christian Literature,* trans. William F. Arndt and F. Wilbur Gingrich (Chicago, University of Chicago Press, 1952), p. 52.
3. Robinson, *Honest to God,* p. 11.
4. Edgar J. Goodspeed, *Paul: A Biography Drawn from Evidence in the Apostle's Writings* (Nashville, Tennessee, Abingdon, 1947), p. 18.
5. Vallee, *Anatomy of a Phenomenon,* pp. 148–151.

CHAPTER V

1. Robinson, *Honest to God,* p. 11.
2. Cf. the article by R. O. P. Taylor, "Heaven and the Heavens in the New Testament, a Distinction," *Interpretor,* January, 1919, pp. 106–112.
3. *Time,* "A Fresh Look at Flying Saucers," August 4, 1967, p. 33.
4. Cf. Albert Einstein, *The Meaning of Relativity,* 5th ed. (Princeton, N.J., Princeton University Press, 1956). See also Benjamin Harrow, *From Newton to Einstein: Changing Conceptions of the Universe* (New York, Van Nostrand, 1920); Harrow's work includes articles by A. Einstein, A. S. Eddington, and J. J. Thomson. See also the work by Walter Sullivan, *We Are Not Alone,* (A Signet Book: New York, New American Library, 1966), reprint from McGraw-Hill edition. See especially Sullivan's Chapter 16, "Can They Visit Us?" (pp. 225–241), for discussion and references to space travel and Einstein's theory of relativity.
5. Keyhoe, *The Flying Saucer Conspiracy,* pp. 247–262.
6. B. H. Arnold, *Intuitive Concepts in Elementary Topology* (Englewood Cliffs, N.J., Prentice-Hall, Inc., 1962), p. 89.
7. Keyhoe, *op. cit.,* pp. 135–136.

8. On February 1, 1966, I sent a letter by registered mail to the Project Blue Book Information Office, SAFOI, Washington, D.C., 20330, U.S.A., containing some of the suggestions discussed here concerning any possible relation between relativity theory, curvature of space, and UFOs, but I received no reply to my letter. Since the administrators of Project Blue Book do not admit having any "firm evidence" of the existence of UFOs, it would, of course, be difficult for them to reply to a letter based on the assumption that they do exist.

9. See the unusual account recorded in Vallee, *Anatomy of a Phenomenon*, pp. 155–157.

10. Bauer, *A Greek-English Lexicon of the New Testament*, p. 70.

11. *Ibid.*, p. 887.

CHAPTER VI

1. Isaac Newton, *Isaaci Newtoni Opera Quae Exstant Omnia*, ed. Samuel Horsley (Londini, Excudebat Joannes Nicols, 5 vols., 1779–1785). "Observations on the Apocalypse of St. John," Vol. V, *Opera*, p. 449.

2. Albert Schweitzer, *The Quest of the Historical Jesus: A Critical Study of Its Progress from Reimarus to Wrede*, trans. W. Montgomery, 3rd ed. (London, Adam & Charles Black, 1954), see especially pp. 222–268, on eschatology.

3. Ritchie Calder, *Science in Our Lives* (newly rev. ed., A Signet Book: New York, New American Library, 1962), p. 24.

4. Cf. James S. Allen, *The Neutrino* (Princeton, N.J., Princeton University Press, 1958). See also Isaac Asimov, *The Neutrino: Ghost Particle of the Atom* (Garden City, N.Y., Doubleday, 1966).

5. William James, *The Varieties of Religious Experience: A Study in Human Nature* (A Mentor Book: New York, New American Library, 1958), 3rd printing; see especially the chapter "The Reality of the Unseen," pp. 58–75.

SELECTED
BIBLIOGRAPHY

The Holy Bible, Revised Standard Version

Altizer, Thomas J. J., *Mircea Eliade and the Dialectic of the Sacred* (Philadelphia, Westminster, 1963).

Bauer, Walter, *A Greek-English Lexicon of the New Testament and Other Christian Literature,* trans. William F. Arndt and F. Wilbur Gingrich (Chicago, University of Chicago Press, 1952).

Bultmann, Rudolf, *Jesus Christ and Mythology* (New York, Scribner, 1958).

Edwards, Frank, *Flying Saucers—Serious Business* (New York, Lyle Stuart, 1966).

Einstein, Albert, *The Meaning of Relativity,* 5th ed. (Princeton, N.J., Princeton University Press, 1956).

Gesenius, William, *A Hebrew and English Lexicon of the Old Testament with an Appendix Containing the Biblical Aramaic,* trans. Edward Robinson, ed. Francis Brown, S. R. Driver, and Charles A. Briggs (Oxford, Clarendon Press, 1959).

Keyhoe, Donald E., *The Flying Saucer Conspiracy* (New York, Holt, 1955).

Noth, Martin, *Exodus: A Commentary,* trans. J. S. Bowden (Philadelphia, Westminster, 1962).

Robinson, John A. T., *Honest to God* (London, SCM Press, 1963).

Sullivan, Walter, *We Are Not Alone.* A Signet Book (New York, New American Library, 1966), reprinted from McGraw-Hill edition.

Vallee, Jacques, *Anatomy of a Phenomenon: Unidentified Objects in Space—A Scientific Appraisal* (Chicago, Henry Regnery, 1965).